NOT ON LOVE ALONE

∞

NOT ON LOVE ALONE

A COOKBOOK

A Year of Delicious Dinners and More for Newlyweds

Jessie Carry Saunders

MARLOWE & COMPANY
NEW YORK

NOT ON LOVE ALONE: *A Year of Delicious Dinners and More for Newlyweds*
Text and Illustrations Copyright © 2005, 2007 by Jessie Carry Saunders

Published by
Marlowe & Company
An Imprint of Avalon Publishing Group Incorporated
245 West 17th Street • 11th Floor
New York, NY 10011-5300

AVALON
publishing group incorporated

Originally published in hardcover in 2005.

Library of Congress Cataloging-in-Publication Data
Saunders, Jessie Carry, 1976-
   Not on love alone : a cookbook : a year of delicious dinners and more for newlyweds / Jessie Carry Saunders.
      p. cm.
   Includes bibliographical references and index.
   ISBN 1-56924-375-1 (hardcover : alk. paper)
   1. Cookery for two. I. Title.

TX652.S287 2005
641.'612—dc22

2005000279

Paperback ISBN-13: 978-1-56924-305-3
ISBN-10: 1-56924-305-0

9 8 7 6 5 4 3 2 1

Designed by Pauline Neuwirth, Neuwirth and Associates, Inc.

Printed in China

Contents

To JS, who is always a pleasure to feed

Acknowledgments

MANY, MANY THANKS TO: Johnny, Mom, Pops, Will, Patty Madsen, Debbie Brown, Pat Stewart, Mary Ellen Van Buskirk, Callie Haines, Isabelle and Ronny Krishana, Weatherly Ralph, Joyce Chang, Simone Vairon, Mag Rochereau, Francoise Payen, Betsy Newell; my editor, Kylie Foxx, my publisher, Matthew Lore, and everyone at Avalon; Pauline Neuwirth of Neuwirth Associates, for the spot-on book design; and Susi Oberhelman, for designing the beautiful cover. And I wouldn't be eating so well or so often without my friends on Bleecker Street at Murray's Cheese Shop and Ottomanelli's Meat Market.

NOT ON LOVE ALONE

Introduction

THIS IS A cookbook for newly married people. It's not a cookbook for newly married people in the way that the *Joy of Cooking* is—that is, it's not an encyclopedic listing of all the food you might ever make in your entire lives. Instead, it's a book about *meals*—about eating together, about feeding your friends, and about having a life at the dinner table, all year round.

A take-out existence is a monotonous one. It makes you sluggish and, if you believe your mother, will give you bad skin. *But,* some argue, *it's easy. We don't have time. We're busy.* Balderdash.

Cooking for yourselves, and sitting down and eating it with each other, is what this book is all about. It doesn't have to be an investment of hours—some of the best meals are prepared in minutes. But sitting down with your honey keeps you happy. It means you talk to each other face to face, and not just on your cell phones. You get to flirt. And eat. Food is love, after all.

And don't I know it.

When my husband, JS, and I first met in college, he pointed out a peculiarity of mine to me. "Whenever you talk about your vacations," he said, "the only thing you ever mention is the food you ate while you were there."

I protested, but he was prepared. He had proof. He reminded me of a trip

I'd taken recently with my parents, to a chalet in the Italian Alps. Some people might have been impressed by the majesty of the mountains, the breathtaking green of the valleys, et cetera, but the only thing I remembered was this small dish of fresh pasta with squash blossoms and butter I'd eaten as part of my dinner. I'd gone on and on about it. What was in it? Could I make it at home? Had I mentioned how good it was?

I blame this food fanaticism on my father. I started in the kitchen at my father's knee. Probably literally—I was a very short kid. Growing up, Pops was the cook in the family, working the huge Garland range in our apartment like a mad wizard. Emphasis on *mad*. My father's explosions at the stove were legendary in our family, making every stereotype out there about Irish temperaments ring true. Adding my mother to the mix was a Bad Idea. Her tentative overtures to help were loudly rebuffed. Somehow, however, I snuck in. Perhaps it was because I was so short. I was soon put to work. One of my first duties was making salad dressing: pouring all the ingredients into a jar, screwing the lid on tightly, and shaking as hard as I could for what seemed like hours. Since those days, Pops and I have cooked very happily together. He gets mad, I calm him down, and everybody eats.

As Pops worked rather late when we were little, my brother Will and I ate his cooking only on special occasions and, in the summer, on vacation. Normally, Will and I ate together earlier in the evening, dining on whatever Mom made for us. Will's little trick was swallowing his peas whole so he didn't have to taste them.

But later in the evening, when Pops got home, he and Mom would eat together—in the dining room!—complete with mood lighting and place mats. Watching two adults eat like this throughout my early childhood made a big impression on me: This is what adults do!

I introduced JS to this habit early on. One summer, he was working in Knoxville, Tennessee, and I flew out to visit him with a hunk of Parmesan, a sack of Arborio rice, and a bottle of good red wine from my parents in my luggage. We sat at his rented kitchen table and ate homemade risotto and drank good wine and everything was right with the world.

So I believe in eating together. JS believes in eating whatever I cook, period, which is a compatible philosophy. I understand it can seem difficult to get it together enough to make a meal and sit down—work, social obligations, important baseball playoff games all intrude—but even a simple menu of soup and salad eaten away from the television will mean twenty minutes of behaving like a couple rather than like roommates.

Of course eating together is not the same as cooking together. Some people are endlessly entertained by chopping carrots, peeling apples, or kneading dough. Some people think those people are absolutely crazy. Sometimes these people are married to each other.

Cooking together, working side by side in harmonious silence, in a cheerful, warm kitchen, is a wonderful fantasy that might play out in some households. But in my experience (father, Irish temper, et cetera) cooks can be cranky when other people stick their oar in. The stove is the cook's stronghold, hostile to invaders, no matter how well-meaning. Cooks like things their way. They want to flip the pancakes, cook the bacon perfectly, squeeze the juice just so.

But as long as they're making that meal for you, why complain? This, I'm sure, is the attitude of JS, the man who asks for guidance when heating a can of Campbell's. In fact, the most important role the non-cook can play is that of cooking enabler—doing everything he or she can to make sure the cook will cook again. Even if the idea of sautéing or steaming gives JS hives, rinsing off some dishes or washing a pot after dinner is the least he can do after the nice dinner he's just devoured. And he looks cute in an apron.

Sometimes JS comes grocery shopping with me. We live right off of Bleeker Street in New York City. Right near us are some of the best butchers, fishmongers, and cheese shops in the country, and as I pop into one and then the other, JS dutifully carries his future dinner around the neighborhood. Then he dutifully carries it up five flights of stairs.

Eating together should never mean all pleasure for one, all drudgery for the other. And, in the brave new age of TiVo, dinner need never be rushed in favor of the game or a rerun of *The Simpsons*. Linger a little.

Enjoy each other. Have a civilized conversation about more than the dry cleaning or the cable repairman. It's a recipe for a happy marriage.

To start you on the way to eternal wedded bliss, foodwise, I've come up with menus and dishes for each month of the first year of marriage. Sometimes I've provided the whole shebang—starter, main course, dessert—but other times I've just suggested things and left the details to your own interpretation. Do you feel like a salad? What about some cheese? How involved you make the meal can be up to you.

Some of the menus are more complicated than others, but they all have one thing in common—they're not fussy. Eating at home is about eating elegantly, but not laboriously. I leave the pyrotechnics to the real chefs in the restaurants— and for sanity's sake, so should you.

Besides, a big part of becoming comfortable in the kitchen is learning what flavors you like, and how to combine them without necessarily relying on your tablespoons or (God forbid) cookbooks. It's about what things smell like, look like, feel like in your mouth when you're tasting them. I hope this book will lead you to that kind of confidence.

NOT ON LOVE ALONE

My Kitchen

∞

NOBODY WORKS UNDER ideal circumstances. As proof, I offer up my stove. It came with my apartment, and I kept it because it fits so well. This is also a kitchen with an eighteen-inch dishwasher, a mini-microwave, and a refrigerator that's only twenty-two inches wide. You can see, in the accompanying drawing (not to scale), its impressive dimensions.

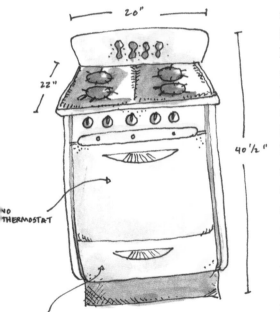

20"

22"

40½"

NO THERMOSTAT

PUT HAND ·and· LIT MATCH IN HERE

Like all stoves, it has some quirks. Its main idiosyncrasy is its lack of a thermostat in the oven, with the added attraction of having no pilot light. I've developed an elaborate process of sticking my hand—holding a lit match—into the belly of the oven to light it; then, after escaping injury, achieving a constant temperature by fiddling with the knob, propping the oven door open with a wooden spoon, and, every once in a while, with the aid of a flashlight, checking the hanging thermometer I've installed on the single rack.

Also, it's on a slight angle. Whether that's the fault of the building or of the oven, I'm not sure. Both have been here for many decades. Every cake comes out just a bit lopsided. That doesn't stop me from baking them, though.

∿ MUST-HAVE KITCHEN ITEMS ∿

HERE ARE SOME things I can't live without in the kitchen. My advice is that you return that panini maker you registered for and get these instead:

UTENSILS

Food mill: Applesauce. Tomato sauce. Any puree that wants just the best parts of the food with the undesirables—seeds, pits, and skin—left behind.

Stainless-steel pepper grinder: For all your fresh peppercorns. It'll last forever and looks great, too.

Bamboo-handled strainer: A cheap investment that comes in handy almost daily

Good heatproof rubber spatulas: For scraping down the sides of hot pans or cold bowls

Mandoline: In its less-expensive incarnation (available at cookware stores like Williams-Sonoma) a mandoline is essentially a slab of plastic with a cutting blade imbedded in it. It's the easiest way to slice potatoes, apples, fennel, celery root, or any other hard fruit or vegetable paper thin.

Good pair of tongs: Almost an appendage to your arm, you can use them to turn chicken cutlets or toss salad greens.

SPRING HINGE HERE

Good chef's knife: Cutting ingredients with a dull blade is not only frustrating, it's dangerous.

Vegetable peeler: Surprisingly versatile. Think of it for curls of chocolate or Parmesan cheese as well as peeling carrots.

NOT ON LOVE ALONE

Kitchen shears: Not just for opening packages any more. Snip parsley, cut up canned tomatoes, matchstick bacon, the uses go on and on.

Instant-read meat thermometer: The only way you'll really know your chicken is done.

POTS, PANS, ET CETERA

My father gave me a deluxe set of All-Clad cookware, one of my favorite presents of all time. If you're wise, you registered for something similar, with heavy bottoms so you don't have the pleasure of scraping burnt food off the pots with Brillo every evening.

In general, you should have:

Large frying pan or skillet (with a lid)
Small frying pan
Nonstick frying pan
Medium-size saucepan (with a lid)
Large pot (at least 6 quarts) with a lid for braising,
  stocks, and boiling water for pasta

Want more? Try:

Cast-iron frying pan
Enameled cast-iron casserole, like those from Le Creuset
Grill pan or griddle that will give you authentic-looking grill lines
Pot specifically for pasta, with a large colander insert for draining

Master Pantry

YOU DON'T NEED me to tell you about all the basic things you should have on hand on a regular basis. I assume you can handle the purchase of your baking powder or granulated sugar. Instead, I've listed and described twenty foods—some quite simple—that I use again and again, and with which you would do well to stock your pantry.

Arborio Rice: The wide world of rice extends beyond the boil-in-a-bag variety. Arborio rice is a very starchy, short-grained rice from Italy, used in one of my favorite dishes: risotto.

Basmati Rice: You can buy this in big bins at the supermarket and use it as your basic, everyday rice. There's no competition between this and converted rice in terms of taste and smell.

Pasta: The ultimate cheap and filling dinner, I like to spend an extra buck or two and get artisanal pastas—which are available more and more everywhere—because of their superior taste and texture. Get a whole bunch of different shapes for different sauces.

Nuts: Particularly pine nuts, whole almonds, hazelnuts, and pecans. All raw and unsalted, they keep best in the freezer, where they'll remain fresh (the oils in nuts go rancid very quickly).

 Lemons: My refrigerator is a forest of half-used lemons. A squeeze of lemon brightens up the dreariest of dishes, and lemons make your kitchen smell wonderful.

Fresh Ginger: Well-wrapped in your fridge, ginger adds a punch of freshness to meals. I like a bit of it grated over sugared pears for dessert.

Shallots: The smaller, violet-colored friend of the onion, their sweetness is perfect for sautéing and for salad dressings.

Onions: I like to have both red and yellow onions on hand. Keep them in a cool, dry place.

Garlic: I usually buy my garlic at the Union Square Greenmarket, where I know the garlic is top quality. When you buy it at your local greengrocer, make sure the head is firm and that there are no obvious shoots poking out of the papery skin—shoots mean the garlic has germinated and has lost some of its oomph.

Greek Yogurt: This is thicker and richer than normal yogurt (even when it's fat-free) and comes in handy as a base for salad dressings, marinades, and sauces. Not surprisingly, it's also nice for breakfast topped with berries and honey.

Unsalted Butter: I use unsalted, or sweet, butter—your basic Land o' Lakes—for baking and general cooking, and occasionally a snooty fancy French butter, higher in milk fat, for impressing people or winning over new friends.

Sea Salt: I talk more about this later, but for salads and finishing off dishes, a sprinkle of real sea salt is the best. Just walk right past the package with the umbrella-toting girl and look for something better.

Kosher Salt: This is my basic cooking salt. It dissolves instantaneously and has a gentle salinity that makes oversalting difficult to do.

Canned Tomatoes: Highest-quality plum tomatoes, canned in Italy, are the cook's salvation ten months of the year. You could use mealy pink hothouse tomatoes in that recipe . . . or a can of perfect plums! The choice is up to you.

Sherry Vinegar: There's a smoky fruitiness to this vinegar that makes it my favorite. I always go for it, leaving the bottles of white and red wine vinegars on my shelf terribly neglected.

Olive Oil: These days, everyone has an olive oil fetish, with fancy gold-wrapped bottles going for more than the price of a decent meal. I avoid the nutsiness, though I do buy a more elegant, fruity olive oil for lettuce salads.

Hazelnut Oil: This sounds obscure, but it's my favorite alternate salad oil—slightly amber, delicate, and just a bit sweet. Use it when you don't want olive oil to be the dominant flavor.

Peppercorns: Sometimes I use black peppercorns, sometimes I'm beguiled by the multicolored variety. Either way, they should be fresh and ground in a good pepper grinder, or used whole. No pre-cracked or ground pepper, please. Such things make me very sad.

presentable. You can also prepare the garlic toasts. If you have a grill pan, that's excellent—you can grill the bread on it and make lovely decorative grill marks. Or you can toast it in the toaster oven. Halve the whole garlic clove and, while the toasts are still warm, rub them with the garlic. Set aside at room temperature.

4. Let the veal cook, turning it occasionally, for 2 hours. Around the 1½-hour mark, turn the heat up slightly (to low, instead of very low) and leave the lid ajar. At the end of 2 hours, the veal should be very tender and cooked through. It should give gracefully under pressure from the back of your fork or stirring spoon.

5. Remove the veal from the pot and place it on a platter (this is just temporary). Pour the cooking juices off into a bowl and reserve (taste for salt content, and add seasoning as needed). Turn up the heat on the pot to medium high. Add the remaining olive oil, and when it's hot, add the shallot and chopped garlic. Stir for a few moments, and when you can smell the garlic, add the mushrooms. Let everything sizzle for a moment, then add the remaining butter on top of the mushrooms. After 30 seconds, give them a good toss for about 5 minutes. (I find that adding the butter on top of the mushrooms prevents the few on the bottom from absorbing all the fat immediately, and thus distributes it nicely.) Add some salt and pepper, to taste. Add the braising liquid back to the pan (you can discard the sorry-looking lemon peel and garlic cloves at this point). Put the roast back in the pot on top of the mushrooms. Put the lid on the pot, then stick it on the back burner on minimum heat for at least 30 minutes.

6. To serve: fish the veal out of the casserole and, starting from either end, try your best to slice it prettily into ⅓-inch slices, though it might fall apart immediately. Cut a toast in half, laying one half slightly on top of the other. Add a serving of veal, then ladle a generous helping of mushrooms and sauce over the top— enough to soak the toast. Add some parsley for color, repeat with the remaining plates, and you're ready to go.

SPECIAL EQUIPMENT: *A good enameled cast-iron casserole or heavy-bottomed pot.*
TIME: *Give yourself at least 3 hours to make this dish, mostly unattended. It can be made ahead and gently reheated at serving time.*
FEEDS: *4 very hungry lumberjacks, or 6 civilized dinner-party guests. The leftovers are great shredded into tomato sauce as a luxurious ragout for pasta.*

Beef and Veal Cuts to Braise

Whenever I visit my butcher's, the venerable Ottomanelli's Meat Market on Bleecker Street, Frank, Jerry, and Peter always stand by patiently as I peruse the refrigerated compartments looking for dinner. Normally, I zoom right past the duck breasts and beef tenderloins in favor of something more . . . everyday.

CHUCK ROAST (BEEF)

This usually means fattier pieces of meat—nothing you would eat rare—that need to sit in a hot bath of braising liquid for several hours in order to become tender. Basically, I mean pot roast. The veal and mushroom recipe is essentially fancier pot roast with a younger cow. Remember what Barbra Streisand says in *Funny Girl* after she eats some French pâté? "It's just chopped liver!"

BONELESS RUMP ROAST (BEEF)

VEAL BREAST

So, which cuts? If you're scouring the supermarket meat case, look for beef chuck or rump roasts, in that order, even better if they're still on the bone. You could also go for a brisket. With veal roast, you could try some shoulder, as in the preceding recipe, or a veal breast, which is very succulent on the bone but occasionally harder to find.

BONELESS SHOULDER (VEAL)

Lace Cookies

Perfect with ice cream, and wonderfully nutty and chewy.

½ stick unsalted butter, softened

⅔ cup packed light brown sugar

⅓ cup white sugar

1 egg

1 cup finely chopped walnuts and pecans

2 tablespoons all-purpose flour

1 teaspoon vanilla extract

1. Preheat the oven to 350°F. Before you start baking, either prepare two nonstick pans by very lightly greasing them, or line two cookie sheets with parchment paper, then grease the paper amply. Don't be shy about this, because to say that these are sticky cookies is an understatement.

2. In a mixing bowl, cream the butter and sugars with a wooden spoon. Mix in the egg. Then add the chopped nuts, flour, and vanilla extract, and stir until just combined.

3. Drop the batter in 1-teaspoon blobs (a soup spoon is good for this) on your prepared cookie sheets. These puppies should be at least 3 inches from each other or you'll have cookie collisions. Throw them in the oven and bake for 10 to 12 minutes, checking after 8 minutes to see that they're not too dark. A dark nonstick pan will make the cookies bake faster than light-colored parchment. Don't underbake them, or they'll never come off the sheet.

4. Pull the cookies from the oven and let cool for several minutes until you pop them off the parchment, or remove them from the nonstick cookie sheet using a very thin spatula. If you need to use the cookie sheet again for another batch, let it cool a few minutes longer, and regrease it if need be (used butter wrappers are very handy for this) before the next round.

SPECIAL EQUIPMENT: *Nonstick cookie sheets are highly useful here, since these cookies are all sugar, but you can use cookie sheets lined with parchment instead.*

TIME: *Barely any at all! 15 minutes, start to finish.*

FEEDS: *This recipe makes 4 dozen cookies, so it depends what sort of binge you're on. If you don't eat them all at once, they will last in an airtight container for several weeks.*

ESSENTIAL COMFORTS

Having eaten many cans of chicken soup and many, many jars of applesauce in my life, I need eat no more. You don't need to, either. The real deals—the stuff you make yourself on a Sunday afternoon—are so far removed from the pale supermarket imitations that once you taste them, you won't go back. The bonus? They're almost impossible to mess up.

Chicken Noodle Soup, or Cure for the Common Cold

When you have the midwinter sniffles, eating chicken soup is definitely more fun than downing Robitussin or Nyquil, and probably better for you, too. The best part about the following recipe (and the applesauce recipe as well) is that it freezes like a champ and is always ready when you need it.

This is my mother's recipe and she hates celery, so there's no celery in the finished product (she throws it away after the chicken broth is done). But if you're partial to celery, please feel free to add some in at the end. Just know my mother wouldn't approve.

Several sprigs fresh flat-leaf parsley

Several sprigs fresh thyme

Bay leaf

15 peppercorns

5 lbs. chicken parts—wings, backs, necks—including a whole chicken breast on the bone

3 carrots, peeled and cut into 3-inch sections

2 celery stalks

1 large onion, peeled

2 whole cloves, stuck into aforementioned onion

1 clove garlic, in its papery skin

2 cups dried egg noodles

1 tablespoon kosher salt

A bit of chopped fresh flat-leaf parsley, to taste

NOT ON LOVE ALONE

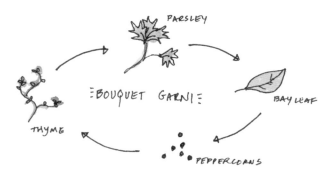

1. Make a bouquet garni: Cut a square of cheesecloth large enough to contain the parsley, thyme, bay leaf, and peppercorns, then cut a longish length of kitchen string and tie the cheesecloth closed like a little hobo bag. Leave a long end of string that you can tie to the handle of your stockpot. Set it aside.
2. Put the chicken in your stockpot along with all the vegetables. Tie the bouquet garni leash to the pot and let the herbs join the fun. Add cold water to the pot until the ingredients are covered by at least 1 inch of water. Fire up the stove.
3. Bring that baby to a boil, then turn it down to the barest simmer. As the pot is coming up to a boil and for about the first 30 minutes, the stock will create a scummy foam. Be diligent and skim it off with a spoon until it ceases.
4. Simmer the stock for 2½ to 3 hours, uncovered. About an hour and a half into the cooking, remove the chicken breasts and keep them covered until you need them. Add more water as necessary to keep the ingredients covered. And keep on skimming—there's no more scum, but plenty of yellow chicken fat rises to the top of the broth. Do this with a soup spoon every 20 minutes or so, particularly if you're planning on eating the soup the same day.
5. Strain the soup through a cheesecloth-lined sieve into a large bowl or another large pot. Save the carrots, but discard everything else from the stockpot.
6. To finish the soup, heat the strained stock to a boil, and add the egg noodles and kosher salt. While the noodles are cooking, slice the carrots into ¼-inch rounds and skin and tear the reserved chicken breast into generous bite-size pieces. As the noodles finish cooking—they'll take only 5 to 7 minutes—turn down the heat to low and add the carrots and chicken. Taste for salt.
7. Ladle the soup into bowls, adding a punch of green with some chopped parsley if you're so inclined.

SPECIAL EQUIPMENT: *Cheesecloth, kitchen string, and a stockpot.*
TIME: *An afternoon, but almost entirely unattended*
FEEDS: *The 2 of you 4 or more times over the course of the month if frozen*

Variations on a Chicken Soup Theme

∞

MAKING YOUR OWN chicken stock sounds like something only preten- tious home cooks would do, but it's very easy. In fact, the Chicken Noodle Soup recipe through step 5—minus the salt and the garlic clove—is exactly that. Making homemade chicken stock is worth it, particularly when the chicken stock is front and center, as it is in a soup.

My favorite way to make it is in my pressure cooker. The ingredients used in Chicken Noodle Soup, are too copious for the average pressure cooker, but if you halve everything, you can have home- made chicken stock in less than an hour, and it's always crystal clear. You don't even have to go to the trouble of the bouquet garni—you can just toss everything in the pot willy-nilly. Ohhhh, and I adore my pressure cooker, which reminds me . . .

How I Learned to Love My Pressure Cooker:

Everybody thinks that if you use a pressure cooker, it's going to blow up, probably in your face. It happens in the movies, after all—doesn't Audrey Hepburn explode her dinner in *Breakfast at Tiffany's*? Yes, the consensus is, if you own a pressure cooker, you're asking for it.

Potatoes Three Ways

POTATOES ALIGOTE (PAGE 32)
POTATOES CRIQUE (PAGE 34)
ROASTED POTATOES WITH SHALLOTS AND TOASTED WALNUTS (PAGE 35)

&

WINTER SALADS AND A SELECTION OF
GOAT CHEESES (PAGES 36 AND 38)

&

SIMPLE CITRUS DESSERTS (PAGE 39)

True Love

DOUGHNUT BITES WITH CHOCOLATE GANACHE FILLING (PAGE 40)

&

CHAMPAGNE AND OTHER BUBBLIES (PAGE 42)

Potato Family Tree

∞

IT SHOULD COME as no surprise to hear that not all potatoes are created equal. Wait—that makes it sound as if I'm potato prejudiced. Perhaps I should say that all potatoes are special, in their own way.

Certainly you're familiar with the Idaho, or russet, potato, the floury giant of the tuber kingdom. High in starch, russets and their relatives are perfect for baking, deep-frying, and mashing.

On the other end of the spectrum, the basic white cooking potato is higher in moisture and lower in starch, giving it the sobriquet *waxy*. It's perfect for boiling and roasting. Though the white potato is humble, it counts among its cousins the very chic fingerling varietals, including Russian Banana Fingerlings and French *rattes*. Then there are new potatoes—so cute, but in fact they're just the immature version of good old white potatoes.

In between, we find the golden mean of potatoes: Yukon Gold, the butter-colored, round variety that performs as well in starchy recipes as it does in waxy ones. Consider it a gift from the potato gods.

Then, of course, there are exotic potatoes, like purple potatoes from Peru, which make an intriguingly colored mashed potato and look great mixed in with other potatoes in a roast. Visit your local farmers' market in the fall for a crash course in unusual varieties. And if that doesn't scratch your potato itch, you can always airlift them in. Wood Prairie Farm (www.woodprairie.com), an organic potato farm in Maine, boasts a potato-of-the-month club for the true tuber fanatic.

POTATOES THREE WAYS

Potatoes Aligote

Despite your newlywed glow, yours isn't the first perfect marriage. Indeed, I contend that the first perfect marriage wasn't even between a man and a woman, but between a potato and a cheese—Potatoes Aligote, an old-fashioned French peasant food from a region called the Auvergne, located in the Massif Central.

1 generous lb. Yukon Gold potatoes

½ cup milk

4 tablespoons butter

½ lb. semisoft cow's-milk cheese, such as Laguiole, Cantal, or Tomme, cut into small pieces (you can also use Gruyère, Swiss, or fontina in a pinch)

Kosher salt and pepper, to taste

A healthy sprinkling of snipped fresh chives

1. Peel and quarter the potatoes, put them in a large pot of cold, salted water, and bring them to the boil. Boil until tender, about 15 to 20 minutes. Drain.
2. Remove the potatoes from the pot and, using a ricer (an essential and cheap kitchen implement for those who like potatoes), rice them back into the pot. (Alternatively, you can return all the potatoes to the pot and mash them with a hand masher.)
3. Meanwhile, heat the milk and butter in a small bowl in a microwave or in a small pan on the stovetop until the milk is hot and the butter has melted. This should only take a minute or two, either way.

best dressings have very few ingredients, and once you've developed a light touch, they are mixed more by taste than by measurement. I like a ratio of about 4:1 for oil to acid.

Some of my favorites: hazelnut oil, fresh lemon juice, salt and pepper; heavy cream, fresh lemon juice, salt, and pepper; garlic-infused olive oil, chopped fresh flat-leaf parsley, sherry vinegar, salt, and pepper; olive oil, a bit of Dijon mustard, sherry vinegar, fresh lemon juice, salt, and pepper.

I suggest trying any of the winter salads here with a small selection of goat cheeses (see page 38).

Winter Salad Combinations:

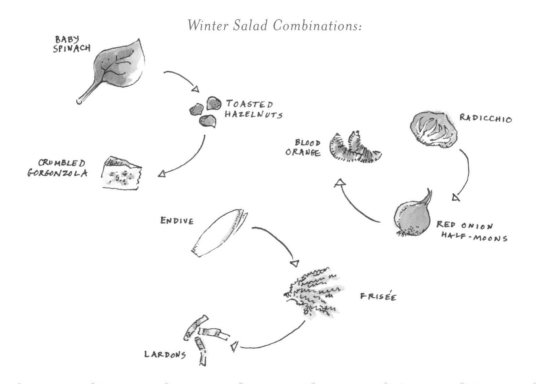

BABY SPINACH

TOASTED HAZELNUTS

CRUMBLED GORGONZOLA

BLOOD ORANGE

RADICCHIO

ENDIVE

RED ONION HALF-MOONS

FRISÉE

LARDONS

Fromage!

a Cheese Play in Five Acts

ACT ONE: *Chèvre, Mon Amour*

SCENE: *Murray's Cheese shop, corner of Cornelia Street and Bleecker Street, New York City. Daytime. J stumbles in, carrying large, unwieldy bag of groceries. CIELO stands behind the counter, cool as a cucumber.*

J, *wedging her bag between the Parmigiano Reggiano and the chorizo display*. Whew. Hi, Cielo. (*J examines the display case of cheese.*) Could I please have . . . (*Indecision sets in.*)

CIELO, *cheerfully*. Hello, lady. What are we making for dinner?

J. Oh, just some potatoes and salad . . . I dunno . . . maybe some goat?

CIELO, *gesturing toward the Selles-sur-Cher*. This is very good today. Nice, ripe. (*He forks over a sample.*)

J, *eating*. Mmmmm . . . (*She eats some more.*) Mmmmm, mmmmm . . .

CIELO. How much do you want, thirty pounds?

J. Yeah, but I forgot my wheelbarrow.

(black out)

CELLES - SUR - CHER

CHEVROT

MONTRACHET

TOMME de CHEVRE

CROTTIN

⚜ SIMPLE CITRUS DESSERTS ⚜

February: It's freezing. My socks are always wet from the slush puddles at the corners. It's pitch black at four o'clock in the afternoon. Is it any wonder that I get lost in Dickensian fantasies of decidedly Victorian illnesses I've suddenly contracted? I latch on to any chronic condition that sounds as if I'm in dire need of a fainting couch and a mustard plaster. Pleurisy? Lumbago? Consumption? Bring 'em on.

That's why citrus desserts are a good idea in February. Vitamin C seems a worthy foe of all diseases Victorian, and citrus brings a sparkling brightness into a world gone into deep freeze. They need not be complicated; in fact, the closer the fruit remains to its original state, the better. And the preparation should take no longer than ten minutes, which should leave you just enough strength to crawl back to the fainting couch and eat dessert.

Some suggestions:

- ❧ Orange sections sprinkled with cinnamon

- ❧ Grapefruit sections roasted with brown sugar

- ❧ Orange sections with caramel sauce over vanilla ice cream

- ❧ Grapefruit sections and fresh mint, sautéed in butter and sugar, served over a dollop of mascarpone cheese

- ❧ Mixed citrus salad sprinkled with sugar and Grand Marnier

See Sectioning an Orange on page 101 for tips on preparing citrus fruit.

TRUE LOVE

You might notice a lack of dinner in this menu, but here's some good advice: nobody wants to do dishes after dinner on Valentine's Day. So do yourselves a favor and go out to eat, and save the dessert and some bubbly for later.

Doughnut Bites with Chocolate Ganache Filling

Nice underwear . . . check; Champagne . . . check; mood lighting . . . check; doughnuts . . . check? I'm not talking Dunkin' Donuts here. These are tiny triangles of deep-fried dough filled with chocolate ganache, a very elegant bite for two to enjoy with a glass of Champagne.

You can make these doughnuts ahead and seal them in an airtight container for when you come home.

FOR THE DOUGHNUTS:

1 cup warm water

2 (¼-ounce) packets active dry yeast

3½ tablespoons superfine sugar

2 sticks butter, softened

5 large eggs

4 cups all-purpose flour

1 teaspoon salt

Neutral vegetable oil (such as canola or safflower) for frying

FOR THE CHOCOLATE GANACHE:

7 ounces semisweet chocolate

¾ cup heavy cream

1 teaspoon unsalted butter, softened

FOR DUSTING THE DOUGHNUTS:

Superfine sugar

1. Put the warm water, yeast, and a teaspoon of the sugar in a little bowl until the yeast wakes up—somewhere between 5 and 10 minutes. When you check the yeast, it should be nice and foamy.

MARCH

A Fish Tale

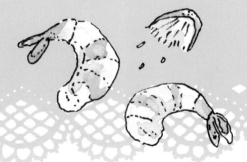

A Fish Tale

ONE OF THE first things I learned about JS when we moved in together was that he had a fondness for fish sticks. And when I say fondness, I really mean obsessive love bordering on the unhealthy. He can eat an entire box in one sitting—which I'm sure is not the recommended serving size on the back of the package—and he doesn't even use tartar sauce. (Isn't that fish-stick sacrilege?)

While the occasional fish stick does send me on a Proustian journey to my days in the third grade, in general I'm wary of the industrially formed fish stick, in the same way I'm repelled but beguiled by that greatest of all mystery foods, the Chicken McNugget. Fish, particularly, is best when left alone, allowed to be itself with a minimum of human intervention. It was with this principle in mind that I conceived my first menu for this month.

It's a good thing to know how to cook fish properly, and it's not scary or hard. It just involves a bit of attention for a very short period of time. I've included a simple recipe for Fish Fillets Meunière, along with a green bean salad. You can serve the green bean salad as a separate first course, but I like to serve it alongside the fish, particularly in the spring and summer, when the cool crunch of the salad is a welcome counterpoint to the pan-hot fillet. I've also included my favorite ways to poach shrimp, steam mussels, and sear scallops, three versatile seafood dishes that are open to a thousand interpretations—if you follow a few rules.

So now, in between bouts of fish sticks, JS will indulge in a little well-cooked flounder or a steamed mollusk or two, prepared not by the Gorton's Fisherman but by yours truly.

Go Fish

GREEN BEAN AND HAZELNUT SALAD (PAGE 48)
&
FISH FILLETS MEUNIÈRE (PAGE 52)
&
LEMON GINGER TART (PAGE 54)

~

Seafood—The Greatest Hits Collection

BEST POACHED SHRIMP (PAGE 57)
&
BEST STEAMED MUSSELS (PAGE 58)
&
BEST SEARED SCALLOPS (PAGE 59)

⌒

Green Bean and Hazelnut Salad

I'm not crazy about hazelnuts in desserts—well, except for a dollop of Nutella now and then—but I absolutely adore them in savory dishes, particularly with green beans. You can get hazelnut oil at a gourmet shop and keep it in the fridge so your investment doesn't go rancid on you. It's a lighter, sweeter alternative to olive oil, but if you don't have it, don't fret—olive oil works just fine.

1 lb. green beans, trimmed (if you are having a dinner party, you could splurge for tiny *haricots verts*)

¼ cup raw hazelnuts

1 small shallot, minced

Small handful of fresh flat-leaf parsley, chopped fine

2 tablespoons hazelnut oil

Sea salt and pepper, to taste

1. Blanch the green beans: Put the beans in a shallow saucepan, cover them with cold water, and add a good pinch of salt. Bring them to a boil over lively heat until the beans are still firm but not crunchily raw, about 4 minutes, depending on the heftiness of your beans. The best way to test them is to taste them; alternatively, pick one up by its end and hold it horizontally. If it's ever so slightly relaxed (a small bend, not a total collapse), the beans are done. Drain and immediately run under cold water, tossing to cool them (this is very important if you want to keep them bright green).

2. While the beans are cooking, toast the hazelnuts. This is easily done in a few minutes in a 400°F toaster oven. Or you can swirl the hazelnuts in a dry, heavy-bottomed pan over high heat until they're fragrant and toasty. Either way, keep a close eye on them so they don't burn. Turn them out onto a cutting board and give them a medium-rough chop, removing any hazelnut skin that falls off (don't worry too much about this—it's more for aesthetics than anything else).

3. Put the cooled beans, hazelnuts, shallot, and parsley in a bowl with the hazelnut oil and toss to combine, adding salt and pepper to taste. It's best to keep this at room temperature if you're going to serve it anytime soon; if you want to store it overnight, it should go, covered, into the refrigerator.

TIME: Less than 10 minutes; it can be made ahead and kept at room temperature for several hours
FEEDS: 2 to 4 people

⌣ VEGGIES & NUTS IN FRIENDSHIP ⌣

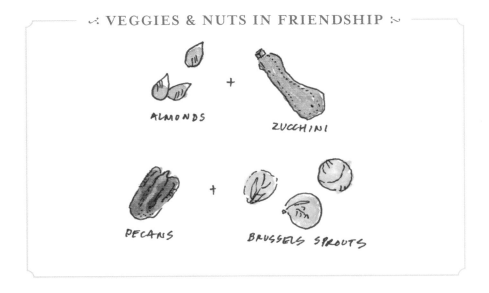

ALMONDS

+

ZUCCHINI

PECANS

+

BRUSSELS SPROUTS

A Trip to the Fishmonger

$\mathscr{A}$T ANY HIGH-end supermarket or gourmet store, there's sure to be someone behind the fish counter who can help you make sense of the seafood buffet in front of you. I like to take JS shopping with me to my local fish store, Citarella's, because (a) he's very good at carrying packages, and (b) he's always astounded by the display. He thinks to ask the fishmonger questions I don't, such as "What the hell is a razor clam?" and "How do you cook rock shrimp?" and "Can you give me a slice of tuna so I can eat it raw right now?" (The answer to the last question was yes, by the way.)

The lesson here is *ask questions*. The people behind the counter are always happy to answer them, because they work with fish all day and have a bit of knowledge on the subject

5. Preheat the oven to 350°F. Take out the dough and let it sit in your warm kitchen for 5 minutes. On a floured surface, roll the dough out with a floured rolling pin, trying to keep it even in thickness, until you have a respectable circle that almost covers the bottom of your 9-inch pan. Then, draping the dough over a long spatula, transfer it to the tart pan and help it fill out the rest of the way by patting it in the pan, starting at the center and radiating out and up the sides of the pan. Not very pretty, but no one's going to see it anyway. Try to build up the sides a bit over the edge of the pan, since the crust will shrink slightly in baking. Prick it with a fork a few times.

6. Line your nice crust with parchment paper and place some dried beans or rice, or a fancier version of pie weights, in there. Bake until the edges of the crust are lightly golden, about 20 minutes. Take the tart shell out of the oven, remove the parchment (careful with the beans!), and let cool.

7. Turn down the oven to 325°F.

8. While the tart shell cools, make the filling. This includes one of my least favorite kitchen tasks, zesting lemons. But go ahead, zest them, then place the zest and the cream in a medium-size bowl and set aside.

9. Slice the pith (the white stuff) off your denuded lemons and throw away, as it's very bitter. Slice the lemons widthwise (be sure to remove any pits!).

10. Throw the slices in a blender (or your freshly washed food processor) with the eggs, egg yolks, sugar, and tiny pinch of salt. Blend.

11. Strain the mixture into the bowl with the cream and whisk until combined. Put the cooled tart pan on a cookie sheet so if there's any spilling, you won't have to clean the oven later. Pour the filling into the tart shell and carefully transfer it to the oven. Bake for 35 to 45 minutes, until the filling in the center jiggles just slightly when encouraged. Remove from the oven, let cool, and eat.

SPECIAL EQUIPMENT: *A food processor (plus a blender if you have one); a rolling pin (you could use a wine bottle as a substitute); a 9-inch tart pan (a removable bottom is an extra bonus); parchment paper; and pie weights, by which I mean a $1.39 bag of dried beans.*
TIME: *You'll need an afternoon, because the pastry has to rest after you make it. But lots of the time is unattended.*
FEEDS: *10, comfortably*

SEAFOOD—
The Greatest Hits Collection

Sometimes the best things in life are the most difficult to cook. This is certainly true of shrimp, mussels, and scallops, all of which can be sublime if cooked properly but are often done in by some ham-handed chef. Think of that poor mussel, giving up its life to metamorphose into one of those rubber superballs you get out of a gumball machine. Or that sad sad shrimp that now seems to be made of damp recycled newspaper. Well, fret no more over our briny friends. Below I've included my three foolproof ways to cook shrimp, mussels, and scallops. The only rule is, please follow my rules exactly. And don't walk away from the stove.

⌣ THINGS TO DO WITH POACHED SHRIMP ∾

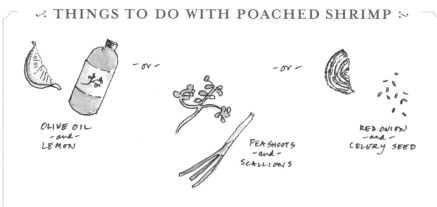

OLIVE OIL
-and-
LEMON

- or -

PEA SHOOTS
-and-
SCALLIONS

- or -

RED ONION
-and-
CELERY SEED

Note: Fish Smell Be Gone! A small dish of vinegar placed in your kitchen after your fish feast will rid the room of any lingering aromas.

APRIL

Early Birds

Early Birds

W HEN JS AND I go to the green market at Union Square early on Saturday mornings in late April, the farmers are just starting to get in a few local spring vegetables. Instead of the usual complement of carrots, beets, and old sweet potatoes, we begin to see hints of the bounty to come: ramps and spring garlic, for instance, or the beginnings of a few strawberries here and there.

Of course, some of the most evocative springtime vegetables don't find purchase in Hudson River Valley farms in April, but come to NYC from sunny California. My favorite of these is the artichoke, available year-round but best in the early spring, which is its actual season. In the first menu I've included both artichokes and another spring favorite, asparagus. The other elements are the best, tenderest pork roast you'll ever eat, and an old family recipe—a chewy, featherweight meringue cake bolstered by whipped cream and strawberries.

Speaking of old family recipes, early birds are often hungry after foraging at the green market and carrying their purchases twenty blocks and up five flights of stairs. On my mother's side, I am the happy inheritor of dozens of old-fashioned Pennsylvania Dutch breakfast recipes, three of which I give here. There's nothing chic or trendy about these dishes—which is what makes them so good.

Spring Forward

HERB-BRAISED ARTICHOKE HEARTS AND PEAS (PAGE 64)

&

ROASTED ASPARAGUS (PAGE 65)

&

PORK LOIN BRAISED IN MILK (PAGE 68)

&

NONNA'S WRONG WAY TORTE (PAGE 72)

~

Mom vs. Aunt Debbie

NANNY'S APPLESAUCE CAKE (PAGE 76)
NANNY'S SCOTTISH CREAM SCONES (PAGE 77)
NANNY'S CINNAMON STICKY BUNS (PAGE 78)

SPRING FORWARD

~

Herb-Braised Artichoke Hearts and Peas

Braised artichokes are delicious but somewhat muted in color. When you add the peas at the very end, they add a nice punch of green.

¼ cup olive oil

6 artichokes, prepped (see Conquering Artichoke Hearts, page 66)

1 clove garlic, slightly crushed but still in one piece, peeled

½ cup mixed chopped fresh flat-leaf parsley and mint

¼ cup chicken stock

Kosher salt and freshly ground pepper, to taste

1 cup high-quality frozen peas

Good crusty bread for serving

1. In a heavy-bottomed saucepan with a tightly fitting lid, heat the olive oil until shimmering. As it's heating, cut the artichoke hearts into quarters. Once the oil is hot, add the garlic clove and let it cook until fragrant, about 30 seconds. Then add the artichoke hearts.
2. Swirl the hearts around in the oil, then add all the parsley and mint, plus the chicken stock. Give it a good pinch of kosher salt and a grinding of pepper, then cover the pot, turn the heat down to low, and let the artichokes cook for 20 minutes.
3. At the end of 20 minutes, test the hearts for doneness (the tip of a paring knife should slide right through them). If you're satisfied, throw in the peas (if you can find fresh peas, you can use them instead—if you use them the day you buy them. Otherwise fresh peas get really mealy really fast). Put the lid on for a minute or two more, so that the peas heat through and get some of the herb flavors. You can serve this hot or at room temperature, but whatever you do, serve it with plenty of crusty bread to sop up all the sauce.

~

TIME: *1 hour, including a leisurely whittling down of the artichokes*
FEEDS: *6 as a side dish or a first course*

Roasted Asparagus

A quick and flavorful springtime dish.

1 lb. asparagus, trimmed	3 tablespoons olive oil
Zest of ½ lemon	Sea salt, to taste
3 tablespoons fresh flat-leaf parsley	

1. Fill a large, deep-sided skillet partway with salted water and bring it to a boil. Add the prepared asparagus and blanch for 2 minutes, then immediately drain and run under cold water to stop the cooking. Alternatively, have a large mixing bowl of ice water standing by in which to plunge the blanched asparagus.
2. Preheat the oven to 500°F.
3. Toss the blanched asparagus with the lemon zest, parsley, and olive oil. Sprinkle on some sea salt to taste. Lay out the asparagus on a rimmed cookie sheet. Place the sheet in the oven and roast the asparagus for 5 to 7 minutes, or until the buds just start to turn color but the stalks remain a vibrant green. Remove from the oven and serve immediately, or at room temperature.

TIME: *15 minutes or more, depending on how fancy you get with the asparagus (see Prepping Asparagus, page 71)*
FEEDS: *6 as a side dish*

Conquering Artichoke Hearts

ARTICHOKES ARE DELICIOUS—but daunting at first. We ate them all the time growing up, but I never paid much attention to how to cook them, so when, as a teenager, I finally looked them up in Julia Child's *Mastering the Art of French Cooking,* I was surprised to find it involved a lot of lemon juice and yards of cheesecloth. Talk about a production.

Since then, I've boiled them, I've steamed them, I've fried them, I've braised them. JS is still partial to an artichoke at room temperature with a simple vinaigrette to dip the leaves in, and there's no more preparation needed than snipping off the tips of the daggerlike leaves and boiling them in acidulated water (this is where the lemon juice comes in) for 30 to 40 minutes.

But to get to the, er, heart of the matter, carving up an artichoke is a bit more complicated.

1. First, remove the bottom three rows of leaves, snapping them backward and pulling them off. Rub this naked area with the cut side of a lemon half.

2. Then, with a large chef's knife, slice off the entire top part of the artichoke, right down to the point where you've denuded the thing. Cut off the stem entirely. Rub the whole thing with the lemon.

3. Using a paring knife—or even better, a boning knife, which is longer and very flexible—begin to carve away any green from the bottom and any evidence of leaves from the top of the artichoke heart. You will be left with a lightly chartreuse, potato-firm disk about an inch and a half thick and 4 inches in diameter.

4. Now to tackle the worst part, the needlelike choke. This can get a bit

messy, so do it over a bowl on your workspace or over the garbage can. Inserting the tip of the paring knife in the flesh of the artichoke just below the edge of the choke, cut in a circular motion to lift the choke out in one piece. The idea is to save as much of the heart as possible while ridding yourself of the inedible choke. Toss the quills and rub again with lemon. You've survived!

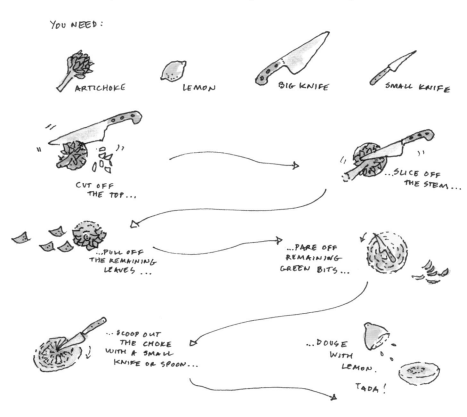

;THE ELUSIVE HEART of the ARTICHOKE ;

YOU NEED :

ARTICHOKE   LEMON   BIG KNIFE   SMALL KNIFE

CUT OFF THE TOP...

...SLICE OFF THE STEM...

...PULL OFF THE REMAINING LEAVES ...

...PARE OFF REMAINING GREEN BITS...

... SCOOP OUT THE CHOKE WITH A SMALL KNIFE OR SPOON...

...DOUSE WITH LEMON.

TADA !

Pork Loin Braised in Milk

This is a very traditional Italian dish that sounds a little curious before you try it. The principle is very simple, and the major ingredients are two: a pork loin and milk. You can experiment with flavoring the milk, adding lemon peel, or sage, or more garlic than I've done here, but I recommend keeping it simple, because this pan sauce, though a bit homely, is one of the tastiest in the world.

One more note: I make this dish with half-and-half because modern pork is bred very lean and therefore the sauce can use the extra milk fat. But you can certainly get delicious results using whole milk instead.

2 tablespoons unsalted butter

1 tablespoon neutral vegetable oil (such as safflower or canola)

Salt and pepper

3-lb. piece of pork loin, weighed with the ribs still attached, then de-boned and tied, with the bones included (or a 2½-lb. pork

loin roast, with a ½ lb. portion of pork short ribs or a small rack of baby back ribs)

1 clove garlic, crushed and peeled

Bay leaf

3 cups half-and-half

Good, crusty bread or basmati rice, for serving

1. Heat the casserole over medium-high heat, and add the butter and vegetable oil. (The bit of vegetable oil will keep the butter's milk solids from burning.) Salt and pepper the pork loin and the ribs, then add the pork loin to the pot and give it a good crusty browning, probably about 12 to 15 minutes total. Regulate the heat if, despite precautions, the butter is looking a little dark. When you're satisfied with the golden goodness of your pork, take the loin out and put it on a plate. Set it aside for a moment.

2. Drop the ribs in the pan and begin to brown them, along with the garlic clove and the bay leaf. When the ribs have gotten a little color, return the loin to the pot. Add 1 cup of the half-and-half, bring to a boil, then cover the pot and turn the heat down to the barest minimum.

3. You should turn the pork every 20 minutes or so, for even cooking and to see how the sauce is progressing. After an hour, the half-and-half will have cooked down quite a bit, forming a rich, butter-colored, custardy sauce. Add another cup of half-and-half at this point, bring it back to a

NOT ON LOVE ALONE

Nanny's Scottish Cream Scones

*M*y *Aunt Debbie told me that my Grandma Baker, Nanny's daughter, put three stars by this recipe on her recipe card. I don't think any further explanation is necessary. Except this: don't overmix the dry and liquid components. And by don't overmix, I mean barely mix at all. Think of all the bricklike scones you've choked down at bridal shower teas in your life, and you'll heed well my warning.*

5 tablespoons butter, chilled and cut into ¼-inch cubes, plus a bit of softened butter to grease the cookie sheet

2 cups all-purpose flour

1 tablespoon sugar

1 tablespoon baking powder

½ teaspoon salt

½ cup half-and-half

2 eggs, lightly beaten

1. Preheat the oven to 425°F. Lightly grease a cookie sheet.
2. Sift together the dry ingredients into a mixing bowl, then cut in the chilled butter using a pastry cutter, two forks, or (my preference) your own two hands.
3. Mix together the half-and-half and the beaten eggs, then add the egg mixture to the flour mixture. Mix very gingerly, just until combined. The cardinal rule here is, the less you touch your dough, the more tender your scones will be.
4. Turn the dough out onto a well-floured pastry cloth or a well-floured board. Pat the dough together—try not to knead it at all—then cut it in half with a floured knife. Form each half into a 6-inch round, then cut each round into four pieces. Place them an inch apart on the prepared sheet and bake until golden, about 12 minutes. They come out light and fragrantly eggy. If you can, eat them hot with butter and a robust jam, such as raspberry or blackcurrant; they taste best the day you make them.

SPECIAL EQUIPMENT: *A pastry cloth, if you have it*
TIME: *About 30 minutes*
FEEDS: *8, if each person eats only one scone (not likely)*

Nanny's Cinnamon Sticky Buns

I saved the best for last. This recipe card, when I first looked at it, was particularly cryptic, referring to mysterious "fruit" that went inside. As I never remembered my mother putting any fruit in these, we had a talk. "I think she would put candied fruit in it," said Mom, "but I put pecans in instead." So while it might be inauthentic, I'm recommending the Virginia Carry variation here.

Nanny's treatment of the yeast was also a bit vague. Mom's helpful suggestion? "Call your Aunt Deb in Cleveland."

¼ cup warm water

¼ cup plus ½ teaspoon sugar

1 (¼-ounce) package active dry yeast

5 tablespoons unsalted butter, plus some to grease the baking pans

1 egg

½ teaspoon salt

1 cup whole milk

3 cups all-purpose flour

⅔ cup light brown sugar, plus 1 cup for sprinkling

½ cup raisins (I like golden ones)

⅔ cup pecan halves

1 teaspoon ground cinnamon

4 teaspoons molasses

1. In a small bowl, mix the warm water, ½ teaspoon of the sugar, and yeast. Set it aside to start to come to life and foam, about 5 minutes.

2. In the bowl of a standing mixer, cream 3 tablespoons of the butter with the remaining ¼ cup sugar until smooth. Add the egg and beat until combined. Add the salt, then the yeast mixture (your mixer should be on a very low setting), then the cup of milk. Slowly add the flour, a cup at a time, and mix until the whole dough is completely combined. Stop the mixer, scrape down the sides, then turn the whole mess (it's very slippery and sticky) into a bowl you've greased, maybe with the wrapper from the butter you just used. Cover the bowl with plastic wrap. Set the bowl someplace warm and let it rise for 2 to 3 hours, or until it has doubled in volume.

3. When the dough is ready, prepare two 9-inch round cake pans by liberally greasing them with vegetable shortening or butter. Don't skimp here or you'll have a headache later. Sprinkle ⅓ cup brown sugar over the bottom of each pan and set aside.

NOT ON LOVE ALONE

4. Generously flour the surface where you plan to roll out the dough. Flour your hands, then coddle the dough into deflating, finally turning it out onto the work surface. Remember, flour is your friend here. Dust the top of the dough, cut it in half, and move one portion to the side to deal with in step 7. As best you can, pat, press, and pull the dough into a rectangle about 10 inches by 8 inches. If you've ever played with pizza dough, that's how this dough behaves—if it springs back, coax it into shape.

5. When you've done your best, sprinkle the top—making an effort to cover the whole surface—with ½ cup brown sugar, ¼ cup raisins, ⅓ cup pecans, and ½ teaspoon cinnamon; dot it with 1 tablespoon of the butter. Roll it as best you can from one long edge to the other, like a jelly roll. Then cut it into 1-inch rounds. You should get eight or nine rounds.

6. Place the rounds, touching, cut side up around the rim of one of the prepared cake pans. Cover it with greased plastic wrap and let it rise again at room temperature for 2 hours.

7. Repeat steps 4 through 6 with the second pan (you could also use one larger pan), then clean up the immense mess you've made of your kitchen. Or better yet, guilt your significant other into doing it by going on about the delicious cinnamon sticky buns you're making.

8. Preheat the oven to 350°F.

9. Drizzle the tops of the buns with the little bit of molasses, just for some added depth of flavor. Pop the pans in the oven and bake for 25 minutes, checking after 20. They're done when they're golden brown and have formed a cake in the pan. Pull them from the oven, and immediately upend them onto a serving platter. Wait 5 minutes before devouring them or you'll burn yourself on the hot sugar.

SPECIAL EQUIPMENT: *A standing mixer is useful here, though I doubt Nanny had one. A pastry cloth is also useful for rolling out the dough. Two 9-inch cake pans.*
TIME: *At least 4 hours of unattended time, as you must wait for the dough to rise twice; the actual mixing and baking takes 40 minutes.*
FEEDS: *This recipe makes about 16 sticky buns.*

MAY

Déjeuner sur l'Herbe

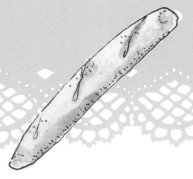

Déjeuner sur l'Herbe

As a kid, I was not a champion picnicker. Ants grossed me out. Bees made me panic. I could never get the hang of planting my glass in the grass so that it remained upright instead of dumped on my lap. As an adult, however, I love to picnic, particularly in the spring. It might have something to do with the fact that, by spring, JS and I have been cooped up in our tiny Greenwich Village apartment (it was advertised as having "Parisian charm," which is code for no bathtub) for well on four months, and look as sickly and pale as downtrodden characters in a Dickens novel.

Picnicking is not something one does well right away. It involves some advance planning, some good luck, and a willingness to improvise. But the ultimate success of a picnic is up to you. Pack carefully. Choose your location wisely. Hide any open wine bottles inside your basket. Read the weather report. Oh, and have a good time. To facilitate your success with the latter, I'm offering a pretty foolproof picnic menu.

And when a full-blown picnic is not in the cards, there's still nothing to stop you from dining alfresco on a park bench. So when you want that picnic feeling without the picnic heavy lifting, consider one of my sandwiches—all very delicious and all very forgiving because they're mayonnaise-free.

NOT ON LOVE ALONE

Picnic Perfect

FRIED CHICKEN, SORT OF (PAGE 84)
&
FRENCH POTATO SALAD (PAGE 87)
CUCUMBER SALAD (PAGE 88)
&
PINWHEEL COOKIES (PAGE 90)

Picnic on a Park Bench

MINI PAN BAGNA (PAGE 93)
&
IMITATION OLIVE'S SANDWICH (PAGE 94)
&
LE SANDWICH MIXTE (PAGE 95)

PICNIC PERFECT

~

Fried Chicken, Sort of

OK . . . this isn't real fried chicken. Real fried chicken involves very careful regulation of large amounts of extremely hot fat. Often the breast meat ends up as dry as can be. In this recipe, you poach the chicken first, so the frying at the end is really just window dressing. One more thing: though I call for a whole chicken so you get both white and dark meat, you could just buy an equivalent weight of thighs and drumsticks and avoid the chance of dry breast meat altogether.

1 quart whole milk

4-lb. chicken, cut into 10 pieces (see note)

2 cloves garlic, peeled

Bay leaf

1 generous pinch kosher salt, plus 1 generous pinch

Neutral vegetable oil (such as canola or safflower), for frying

2 cups all-purpose flour

1 teaspoon cayenne pepper (or to taste)

1. Put the milk in a saucepan and add the chicken, garlic cloves, and bay leaf, along with a hefty pinch of salt. Add a cup of water if the chicken isn't fully covered by the milk. Bring the saucepan to a slow simmer over medium heat and cook until the chicken is tender, about 15 minutes for the white meat and 20 for the dark (you can fish the breast pieces out and set them aside while the dark meat finishes cooking). Give the pot a stir from time to time to prevent any sticking.

2. When the chicken is done, turn off the heat and let the chicken sit tight for a minute while you heat the oil and prepare the flour mixture. Put a clean, dry skillet on the stove (a cast-iron skillet, if you've got it), and add enough vegetable oil so that it comes 1/3 inch up the sides of the pot. Turn the heat on to medium-high.

3. Combine the flour, cayenne, and a big pinch of salt in a zip-top bag, seal, and shake it like you mean it. Then open the bag and add a few pieces of the chicken (you can skin it if you like; in fact, I recommend skinning the breast pieces, as the skin will have shrunk during the poaching) and shake it to coat the pieces well. The oil in the skillet should be shimmering with the heat now, so lay the

Fromage!
a Cheese Play in Five Acts

ACT TWO: *Have Cheese, Will Travel*

SCENE: *A Saturday in late May, lunchtime. J and JS enter Murray's Cheese shop. J is carrying a blanket over her arm. JS is carrying a large cooler, a giveaway from a Mets game circa 1995.* CIELO *stands behind the counter, small smile on his face.*

J. We're going on a picnic. We need unmessy cheese, please. But nothing too hard to slice.

CIELO. Hello, lady. Hello, man. (*He reaches over the counter and gives JS a slice of cheese.*)

JS, *eating with an almost religious fervor.* Mmmmmm . . . we'll take that . . .

CIELO. That's Taleggio. (*He forks over some more cheese to JS.*) And this is a Cantal . . .

JS. OK, some of that, too . . . (*He peers into the display case dreamily.*) What's that? I want some of that one there.

CIELO. That's a nice cheddar from Ireland. (*He smiles devilishly.*) Anything else, man?

J, *interrupting.* See you later, Cielo. I think three cheeses are plenty for a two-person picnic.

CHEDDAR

CANTAL

(*black out*)

TALEGGIO

Pinwheel Cookies

These are a great picnic option—and more original than brownies or chocolate chip cookies—because while they're chocolate flavored, they won't melt and coat your hands, picnic blanket, utensils, et cetera, with chocolate.

1½ cups all-purpose flour	1 egg yolk
½ teaspoon salt	3 tablespoons milk
½ teaspoon baking powder	½ teaspoon vanilla extrace
½ cup butter, softened (keep the wrapper for greasing the cookie sheets)	1 ounce (one square) unsweetened baking chocolate, melted
½ cup sugar	

1. Sift together the flour, salt, and baking powder into a small bowl.
2. In a food processor or with a hand mixer and a large bowl, cream the butter and sugar together; then (through the spout, if using a processor) drop in the egg yolk, followed by the milk and vanilla. Stop the machine and scrape down the sides of the bowl.
3. Add the flour mixture in four portions, blending after every addition. Up-end the bowl onto some waxed paper, and pat the dough into a ball. Divide the ball in half, put one portion back in the food processor bowl, and blend in the melted chocolate. Wrap the dough in separate sheets of waxed paper, then in plastic wrap (and further in tinfoil if you're going to freeze it at this point). They should sit in the fridge for at least 2 hours.
4. On a lightly floured board or pastry cloth, roll the vanilla layer out into a rectangle that's about 6 inches wide and 12 inches long. Carefully move it aside, then repeat with the chocolate layer. Put the chocolate layer on top of the vanilla, lining up the rectangles as well as you can. Then roll them up together lengthwise, as tightly as you can, so you end up with a long, thin cookie log. Wrap the log in plastic wrap and chill for another 30 minutes.
5. Preheat the oven to 350°F and lightly grease two cookie sheets. Unwrap the chilled cookie log and, using a very sharp knife and a light touch, slice into ¼-inch-wide slices. Place the cookies 1 inch apart on the prepared cookie sheets, and bake for 7 minutes, checking them after 5. They're done just after they set—

they shouldn't be browned at all. Transfer the baked cookies to a cookie rack and let cool. You can store them in a tin or another airtight container for several weeks.

SPECIAL EQUIPMENT: *A food processor makes life easier, and a pastry cloth is useful, but not necessary, to roll out the dough.*
TIME: *The dough needs to be refrigerated for several hours after it's made, but you can make it well in advance and freeze it, defrosting it overnight in the fridge. A single-day total would be 3 hours, mostly unattended.*
FEEDS: *The yield here is about 30 cookies. (I never make assumptions about how many cookies a single person can eat in one sitting.)*

PICNIC ON A PARK BENCH:
Eating alfresco every day

I always feel a bit deprived if I don't have a sandwich for lunch. Sometimes I have a salad, but even with a heaping handful of croutons, I'm always grumpy afterward, thinking that everyone who had a sandwich is luckier than I am.

I also like making my lunch and taking it with me, particularly in the spring when I can sit in the park and raise my face to the breeze and munch on a sandwich and watch the city go by. May is when all the crazy people come out of hibernation, so there's a lot to watch.

So I would say, with all due modesty, that I'm a sandwich expert. I've included three recipes for sandwiches that are mayonnaise-free, so all those times you tempted fate by eating that soggy baloney and cheese on camping trips won't come into play here. These sandwiches won't kill you—they'll only make you stronger.

Mini Pan Bagna

Basically a Niçoise salad on a bun. Pack some breath mints along with an extra paper napkin for this one.

½ clove garlic, minced

¼ cup good olive oil

A drizzle of red wine vinegar

Sea salt and pepper

Sturdy, crusty sandwich roll (round or rectangular is better than baguette-shaped here)

1 (3.5-ounce) can of imported Italian tuna

1 small shallot, chopped

½ teaspoon capers, chopped

1 tablespoon chopped fresh flat-leaf parsley

A few black cured Provençal olives, pitted and sliced

1 hard-boiled egg, thinly sliced (optional)

1 small tomato, sliced

Several leaves romaine lettuce

1. In a small bowl, mix the garlic with the olive oil and red wine vinegar. Add some salt and pepper, then set aside.
2. Cut the roll in half and take out some of the soft insides from both the top and the bottom, creating a little bowl for the sandwich filling to sit in.
3. Drain the tuna, then flake it into another small bowl, mixing it with the shallot, capers, chopped parsley, and salt and pepper.
4. Using a teaspoon, drizzle the insides of your sandwich roll with the garlic-oil mixture. Then layer on the tuna fish, olives, sliced egg, tomato, and romaine lettuce. Put the top on the sandwich and give it a good smushing-down. Double-wrap it in plastic wrap, put it in a zip-top bag, and then put it in your bag to take to the office (or wherever you're headed).

TIME: *10 minutes*

FEEDS: *This is the floor model sandwich. Multiply it as many times as you like.*

Imitation Olive's Sandwich

This sandwich, another salad on bread (in this case, Caprese salad), is an imitation of a sandwich I used to buy at college in a local shop called Olive's. I'd buy a sandwich, an oatmeal cookie, and some water, and sit on the large green in the middle of campus and laugh at the students trudging into the library.

A traditional French baguette

A sprinkle of good balsamic vinegar

Good olive oil

Sea salt and pepper, to taste

1 very ripe tomato, sliced

A ball of fresh mozzarella, sliced (ideally you should get the sort that comes swimming in water)

Fresh basil leaves, rinsed and patted dry

Small red onion, peeled and sliced into very thin half-moons

1. Cut the baguette in half. Drizzle each side with a touch of balsamic vinegar and some olive oil. Sprinkle with salt and pepper.
2. Layer the tomato, mozzarella, a few basil leaves, and a few half-moons of red onion on the bottom of the baguette, then top the sandwich with the other half of the bread. Slice in half, so you have two sandwiches. If you're taking it with you, be sure to wrap it in a double thickness of plastic wrap.

TIME: *5 minutes*
FEEDS: *2, if you use the whole baguette*

NOT ON LOVE ALONE

Mock Moroccan

Couscous Salad with Carrots, Pine Nuts, and Orange (page 100)

&

Lamb Tagine with Lemon and Olives (page 104)

&

Lemon Ginger Cookies (page 108)

~

Midsummer Night Snack

Rice Pancakes (page 112)

&

Pop's Grilled Cheese (page 113)

&

Relaxed Blueberries and Vanilla Ice Cream (page 114)

MOCK MOROCCAN

Couscous Salad with Carrots, Pine Nuts, and Orange

The complementary tang of orange, sweetness of carrot, and smokiness of cumin really work well together. They've been incorporated into couscous here, which is not a very Moroccan thing to do at all, but still very good.

4 medium carrots, peeled and trimmed	1 orange, peeled and sectioned
1 cup chicken stock	¼ cup pine nuts, toasted
½ teaspoon light brown sugar	¼ cup chopped fresh flat-leaf parsley
½ teaspoon ground cumin	¼ cup chopped fresh cilantro
Pinch of ground cinnamon	1 tablespoon white wine vinegar
1 tablespoon unsalted butter	3 tablespoons olive oil
Sea salt	Pinch of hot pepper flakes
1 cup dry couscous	

1. Cut the carrots on the bias into ¼-inch-thick coins, and put them in a frying pan with the chicken stock, brown sugar, ground cumin, cinnamon, butter, and a healthy pinch of salt. Bring to a boil over high heat, then turn down the heat to medium-low and cook for 15 minutes, stirring very occasionally. At the end of 15 minutes, turn up the heat to medium and boil away the remaining broth—the evaporating broth will glaze the carrots and intensify the flavors of the spices. This should take 10 minutes. When the carrots are done, turn off the heat and set the pan aside to cool.

2. In a bowl that's large enough to hold all the ingredients, mix the couscous with 1 cup of boiling water. Cover the bowl with plastic wrap (or another bowl) for 10 minutes, then fluff the couscous with a fork. Add the sections of orange, pine nuts, parsley, cilantro, vinegar, olive oil, and pepper flakes, and then the car-

NOT ON LOVE ALONE

rots, scraping out the pan well in order to get all the lovely glaze into the salad. Mix all the ingredients carefully with a spatula, then season with salt—it might need more than you think. I like to serve this with the tender inner leaves of a head of Boston lettuce, which give a lovely crunch and contain the couscous salad prettily inside their curves.

TIME: *45 minutes*
FEEDS: *6 as a side dish*

⌁ SECTIONING AN ORANGE ∿

*A*NY CITRUS FRUIT is easily sectioned. Just cut off the stem end and bottom end so the fruit stands up, then, using a paring knife (or a boning knife, which is thin and flexible and thus perfect for this job), slice the rind off in sections. Trim off any leftover pith, then, holding the orange in your hand, carefully remove the sections in between the membranes.

Marinades, with a Touch of the Exotic

∞

𝒜 MARINADE IS A great way to get a feel for more obscure flavors without committing yourself to a full meal extravaganza, and, in general, marinades are a great way to brighten up supermarket chicken breasts or flank steak. Frankly, these marinades are my equivalent of Old El Paso taco mix. They might not be too authentic or sophisticated, but they taste pretty good.

I always mix everything in a resealable bag and throw the bag out when I'm done, solving the problem of cleanup and refrigerator space at the same time.

1. *Pan-Asian marinade:* This might be the fakest of them all. Put a 1½-lb. piece of flank steak in a gallon bag, and follow that with 1 tablespoon rice vinegar, 1 tablespoon Thai fish sauce, 3 tablespoons soy sauce, ¼ teaspoon Thai chili paste, 2 crushed garlic cloves, and 2 sliced scallions. No need for salt, because the soy takes care of that. Marinate at least an hour before grilling or broiling.

2. *North African marinade:* Sometimes I marinate quails in this in the summertime and then grill them. Put a split chicken breast (on the bone, please) in a gallon zip-top bag with 2 teaspoons toasted whole cumin seeds, 2 crushed garlic cloves, ½ lemon

(squeezed, then tossed in), a good pinch of hot pepper flakes, ¼ cup olive oil, and a hearty pinch of salt. Marinate for ½ hour in the fridge, then broil those babies.

3. *Faux Greek marinade:* This marinade is based completely on tzatziki sauce, which is what douses your souvlaki at summer street fairs. In that same old resealable gallon bag, mix a split chicken breast on the bone with a 6-ounce container of Greek yogurt, 2 tablespoons of chopped fresh dill, the juice of ½ lemon, 3 crushed and chopped garlic cloves, and a pinch of salt. Marinate for ½ hour in the fridge, then broil. As in tandoori chicken, the yogurt really tenderizes the meat.

Lamb Tagine with Lemon and Olives

*T*he name **tagine** *comes from the vessel these stews are cooked in—a glazed ceramic dish, with a long, dramatically curved funnel-shaped lid with a steam vent in the top. It looks a bit like a volcano. You can get the same flavors, however, in a casserole on your stovetop, even if you don't get the same theatrical presentation.*

Lamb tagines are often a bit sweet—one of my favorites is made with lamb and dried figs. But here I've opted for a version with the most basic of Moroccan flavors, lemon and olive.

3 tablespoons olive oil

Kosher salt and pepper

2 lbs. boned leg of lamb, extra fat trimmed, cut into 1½-inch pieces (this makes a firmer stew; if you want softer meat, but more pronounced lamb flavor, get the equivalent amount in boned lamb shoulder)

3 cloves garlic, minced

1 medium red onion, chopped

1 tablespoon freshly grated, peeled ginger

Pinch of saffron threads

1 teaspoon ground paprika

1½ teaspoons ground cumin

A few stems of fresh flat-leaf parsley (leaves removed) and one or two cilantro stems, tied together with kitchen string

1 cup pitted green olives, such as picholines

1 lemon, zested and reserved for juicing

1 egg yolk

2 tablespoons sheep's-milk yogurt or Greek yogurt

¼ cup chopped fresh flat-leaf parsley

Crusty bread for serving

1. In a casserole that can subsequently hold all the ingredients, heat the olive oil over medium-high heat until shimmering. Salt and pepper the lamb, then brown (in batches if necessary) until deep and caramelized on all sides. Be sure to get good color here. Remove the lamb to a plate with a slotted spoon and set aside.

2. In the fat, sauté the garlic until you smell it, then add the chopped onion and give it a good stir, cooking until it's translucent, 3 to 4 minutes. Add the ginger, and cook for a minute more. Then add the saffron, paprika, and cumin, and stir so everything in the pot is evenly distributed. Put the lamb and its juices back in the pot, add the stems of parsley and cilantro, and cover with 1½ cups of water. Bring to a boil, cover the pot, and turn down the heat to the barest minimum.

NOT ON LOVE ALONE

3. Check the lamb after an hour. With the lid slightly ajar, cook it for 15 minutes more, adding a tablespoon more of water if it's looking very dry.

4. Fish the lamb out and put it on a platter for a moment. Discard the limp parsley and cilantro stems. To the juices left in the pot, add the olives and the lemon zest. Stir to combine. Turn off the heat.

5. In a small bowl, whisk together the juice of half the lemon, the egg yolk, and the yogurt, then add it to the juices in the pan, stirring quickly to incorporate. Taste for salt and pepper. Add the lamb back to the pan, turning it in the sauce. You can heat this over the lowest of heats, but don't let it boil, or the egg yolk will curdle and separate. Sprinkle with the chopped parsley, and serve with crusty bread.

SPECIAL EQUIPMENT: *A casserole pot, such as the enameled cast-iron Le Creuset*
TIME: *30 minutes of work time, plus 2 hours of unattended stewing*
FEEDS: *6*

Lamb Cuts

$\mathcal{A}$T OUR WEDDING we served a 1950s favorite, rack of lamb. There's something so elegant about the labor-intensive frenched racks being carved apart, and the rosy round of meat connected to the delicate bone propped on your plate. There's also something so wonderfully barbarian about sitting in your easily stainable pristine white wedding dress and fighting for the last bits of meat off the bone with your fingers and teeth. That's what bridesmaids are for—to help you clean up afterward.

RACK of LAM

At Ottomanelli's, there are three cuts of lamb that I might choose from on an everyday basis. The first would be a few lamb chops; though the most expensive, I still think their flavor is the best. Sometimes Jerry will give me a portion of a leg of lamb, boned, and that's delicious, too, roasted with chilis and garlic in the oven—though that's a bit more special-event, to be honest.

LEG of LAMB

Then there are lamb shanks, which can be braised in Italian flavors or North African flavors, and there is lamb shoulder, which needs to be ruthlessly trimmed (it's very fatty) and used for stews like lamb with white beans or the lamb with vinegar and green beans that's in Marcella Hazan's famous book *Essentials of Classic Italian Cooking*.

LAMB SHANKS

Just ask the butcher—there's a world beyond the lamb chop, and it can be very tasty, indeed.

Moroccan for Intermediates

I THINK I'VE already mentioned that I own a *couscoussière*. I've actually opted to make couscous the crazy way (it involves several steamings, some massaging, and some drying—it sounds like a facial), rather than the sane way, which is to pour hot water in and cover for 10 minutes.

I have also (and I'm a repeat offender here) preserved my own lemons,  which by rights should have been included in the tagine recipe on page 104. This involves slitting lemons with a razor blade, submerging them in brine, and storing them in your refrigerator for at least a month.

There's also a dish called the *pastilla* (it can be spelled fourteen different ways), which involves stewing pigeons and constructing an elaborate, pizza-size layered pie out of phyllo dough. There's a simpler chicken version of it as an hors d'oeuvre on page 208.

So you see, there's a bit of madness involved in becoming more deeply committed to cooking in any one style. Just like a person who has invested in several woks and some obscure Chinese condiments, I've paid my dues to the Moroccan food club. If you're interested in learning more  about more traditional Moroccan food, I suggest you peruse Paula Wolfert's *Couscous and Other Good Food from Morocco*, a bible of Moroccan specialties and traditions.

Lemon Ginger Cookies

This is a much bastardized, very inauthentic Moroccan cookie. There are a lot of absolutely delicious cookies in North African cuisine, but they are tricky to make and involve things like homemade almond paste, rose water, and lots of powdered sugar.

These are a mite easier, but very cute and strongly flavored with lemon and ginger, a favorite combination of mine.

2 cups all-purpose flour

1 teaspoon baking powder

½ teaspoon baking soda

½ cup vegetable shortening, such as Crisco

½ teaspoon salt

½ teaspoon freshly grated lemon zest

½ teaspoon freshly grated nutmeg, or jarred grated nutmeg in a pinch

1 cup sugar, plus extra for rolling the cookies

2 eggs, lightly beaten

2 tablespoons milk

4 tablespoons well chopped candied ginger

¼ cup golden raisins (or ¼ cup slivered blanched almonds)

1. Preheat the oven to 350°F. Grease two cookie sheets.
2. Sift together the flour, baking powder, and baking soda into a small bowl or a large piece of waxed paper.
3. In a mixing bowl that can subsequently hold all the ingredients, use the hand mixer to cream together the vegetable shortening, salt, lemon zest, nutmeg, and sugar until smooth. Add the eggs. In increments, and on low speed, add the flour mixture. This is quite a stiff dough and you will end up with a face full of flour if you're not patient with the hand mixer.
4. When all the flour has been combined, mix the milk into the dough with a wooden spoon. Fold in the chopped candied ginger.
5. Scoop out dough in heaping teaspoons, roll into balls, then give the balls a quick spin in a plate of sugar. Put them on the baking sheet, make an indentation in the top of the balls with your finger, and put a golden raisin in the spaces. (Or,

Not on Love Alone

JULY

Vacation, All I Ever Wanted

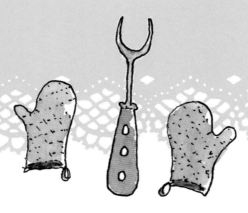

Vacation, All I Ever Wanted

MY PARENTS ARE major Francophiles. In fact, since my father retired, they spend nearly half their time in France, in a house they own in a village in the middle of the boondocks. Of course, the French have a nicer term for "boondocks"—they call it *la France profonde*. What that really means is that there are more goats than people.

Needless to say, it's quite a change from the big city, but they are very happy there, and we (by whom I mean me, JS, and my brother, Will) are very happy to visit them. What do we do all day? We look at the ancient buildings, swim in the local river, read books we haven't gotten to all year, and eat. Boy, do we eat.

I should explain that my father's main hobbies in life are (a) tennis and (b) cooking. In the summertime, I have always been his sous-chef, fixing a first course or chopping some shallots, but it's my pleasure (and JS's, and Will's, and Mom's) to sit back and just eat all the delicious food my father makes. Then wash the dishes afterward.

So in honor of Pop's years of culinary excellence, I'm including a menu of things he always makes for us on vacation.

And since you have to eat the next day, too, I've included a salad that we often have for lunch. It's very flexible and ingredients can be tossed or added as you wish. It's also a light dinner favorite.

Pop's All-Star Summer Revue

SOUPE AU PISTOU (PAGE 118)

&

RIB OF BEEF ON THE GRILL (PAGE 121)

&

POP'S FRIED ZUCCHINI (PAGE 122)
POP'S TOMATOES PROVENÇAL (PAGE 123)

&

POP'S CHOCOLATE SAUCE FOR ICE CREAM (PAGE 125)

Cool Lunch for a Hot Day

SALADE NIÇOISE COMPOSÉE (PAGE 126)

&

APRICOT-THYME CLAFOUTI (PAGE 130)

POP'S ALL-STAR SUMMER REVUE

Soupe au Pistou

As soon as I tell you these are all Pop's recipes, I immediately give one that's not. In fact, this is the recipe of our old next-door neighbor, Simone Vairon. Originally, it was the recipe of her mother, Madame Cogat. But every family in the south of France has a Soupe au Pistou recipe. It's practically the law. This one is very close to my heart—I have a picture of myself at two years old eating this very soup for lunch on the Vairons' terrace.

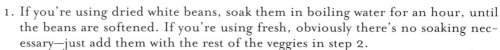

1 lb. fresh white shell beans, or the same amount of dried white beans, such as flageolet, cannellini, or white northern

1 large zucchini, cut into ½-inch dice

3 leeks, white parts only, cut in half and sliced ½-inch thick

½ lb. green beans, trimmed and cut into 1-inch lengths

3 carrots, peeled and cut into ½-inch-thick rounds

1 medium ripe tomato, cut in half

4 Yukon Gold potatoes, peeled and cut into ½-inch dice

1 tablespoon kosher salt

2 large cloves garlic, smashed and diced

1 large handful of basil leaves, torn up

⅓ cup olive oil

¼ lb. small elbow macaroni

Sea salt

Grated Gruyère or Swiss cheese and an old-fashioned French baguette, for serving

1. If you're using dried white beans, soak them in boiling water for an hour, until the beans are softened. If you're using fresh, obviously there's no soaking necessary—just add them with the rest of the veggies in step 2.
2. Put the first seven ingredients, through the potatoes, in the pressure cooker. (If you're using a standard soup pot, add the first six, through the tomato (the potato should be added toward the end of the cooking so it doesn't disintegrate). The pressure cooker should be filled with water up to the two-thirds safety line; the conventional soup pot should be filled with water until the vegetables are

NOT ON LOVE ALONE

Pop's Tomatoes Provençal

A simple summer treat.

4 medium-size ripe tomatoes

2 cloves garlic, minced

2 tablespoons chopped fresh basil

4 tablespoons olive oil

Salt and pepper

1. Preheat your oven to 375°F, or preheat your toaster oven to 350°F.

2. Cut the tops off the four tomatoes and discard. Give the tomatoes a squeeze into the garbage to get rid of some of the seeds. Set them on the counter to see if they'll sit upright. If they roll, cut a small sliver off the bottom to give them a comfortable place to sit.

3. Top each of the tomatoes with a bit of garlic, some chopped basil, and a tablespoon of olive oil. Sprinkle with salt and pepper, then transfer to a small gratin dish where they can fit snugly, or to the tray of your toaster oven (you can line it with foil first for ease of cleanup). Bake them for 20 minutes in the oven, or 15 minutes in the toaster oven, until they're a bit relaxed and juicy, but still standing on their own. Keep warm until you serve.

SPECIAL EQUIPMENT: *These can be made beautifully in the toaster oven, which has the added advantage of not heating up your entire kitchen.*
TIME: *Easily made while you shlurp a glass of rosé*
FEEDS: *4*

Fromage!

a Cheese Play in Five Acts

ACT THREE: *The Old Stinkers*

SCENE: *Early Saturday morning, mid-July. Picturesque town square, filled with vegetable, fish, meat, and cheese stands—a French* marché. *In the middle of the square rests the moving-van-size cheese truck, with a long line of patient shoppers snaking from one end.* POP, J, *and* JS *stand on the line, carrying heavy bags of melons, zucchini, et cetera.* MOM *sits in a nearby café, drinking café au lait and reading the* International Herald Tribune.

J, *standing downwind of the truck, wrinkling her nose.* Whoo! This is a bit strong for 8 AM.

POP. When I die, I want to be laid out in the cheese truck. You won't be able to smell me for a month.

EPOISSES

J. Thanks for that.

JS, *sniffing discerningly.* Which one smells like old shoes?

POP, *cackling evilly.* That's the Reblochon. And it's on my list.

J, *resigned.* And what else?

POP. The Pont L'Évêque. And the Époisses.

JS. It's a good thing we eat outside.

(*black out*)

PONT L'ÉVÊQUE

REBLOCHON

NOT ON LOVE ALONE

Pop's Chocolate Sauce for Ice Cream

This is a family tradition, adapted from Maida Heatter's Book of Great Chocolate Desserts. The original recipe calls for heavy cream, but Pop has always made it with crème fraîche in France. He once had to make it with yogurt, and it was delicious even so—a little zippy, actually!

Serve it over ice cream for the best chocolate sundae ever—the sauce firms up when it hits the cold ice cream, sliding off your spoon like molasses. Sometimes I ignore the ice cream and just eat the sauce.

½ cup crème fraîche or heavy cream

3 tablespoons unsalted butter

⅓ cup sugar

⅓ cup light brown sugar

pinch of salt

½ cup good-quality Dutch-process cocoa powder

In a small saucepan, melt the butter in the crème fraîche over medium-low heat, until the butter is melted and the mixture begins to boil. Add the sugars and stir until dissolved—a minute or two. Add the salt and cocoa powder, and combine with a whisk to prevent any lumps. When it's smooth and shiny, it's ready for the ice cream. You can keep it in the fridge or freeze it if you're not going to use it right away (just reheat it in a double boiler before serving).

SPECIAL EQUIPMENT: *If made ahead and you want to reheat, you'll need a double boiler, or 2 pots that work together as a double boiler.*
TIME: *5 minutes*
FEEDS: *6, copiously*

COOL LUNCH FOR A HOT DAY

Here's the thing: I love salad, but I love salad with things in it. Often, those things are shredded cheese and garlicky croutons. But Salade Niçoise satisfies my jones for variation, without necessarily adding impressive levels of fat and cholesterol. It's light, tasty, and all around, the perfect lunch salad.

Salade Niçoise Composée

I always like to lay out vegetables on top of a base of salad, so people can pick and choose their favorite elements and the heaviest stuff doesn't fall to the bottom of the salad bowl.

FOR THE SALAD:

1 red bell pepper

Head of lettuce, or a mix of lettuces, washed and dried

A handful of fresh basil

1 large (6-ounce) can fancy tuna packed in olive oil from Italy, such as Progresso, drained and flaked

¼ lb. string beans, prepped and blanched for 3 minutes in salted boiling water

2 hard-boiled eggs

¼ lb. new potatoes, boiled and sliced into bite-size pieces

1 large, ripe summer tomato, cut into wedges

FOR THE DRESSING:

2 tablespoons sherry vinegar

1 tablespoon Dijon mustard

⅓ cup olive oil

1 clove garlic, minced

1 teaspoon capers, drained and chopped

1 shallot, minced

Sea salt and pepper, to taste

1. Over an open burner on your stove, roast the red pepper on all sides until charred and black. (Use a pair of tongs to turn it, and before you begin move away any loose papers or other flammables in case of stray sparks. Don't worry—it's not as scary as it sounds.) Place the pepper in a zip-top bag and let it sit for 10 to 15 minutes. Take the pepper out of the bag and, rinsing it off as little as possible, peel and core it. Cut it into slivers.
2. Make the dressing: In a small bowl, combine the sherry vinegar and mustard until smooth, then slowly whisk in the olive oil. You should have a lovely emulsified vinaigrette. Add the garlic, capers, and shallot, and season to taste with salt and pepper.
3. Tear the lettuce into bite-size pieces; do the same with the basil. Toss to mix. Add half of the dressing—just enough to very lightly coat the leaves.
4. To serve, heap the lettuce and the basil leaves in the center of a large platter. Put the tuna on top, then arrange the veggies and egg wedges around the edge in groups so it looks like something out of a painting. Drizzle with some extra dressing. Then say in French, "*Voilà!*"

SPECIAL EQUIPMENT: *Nothing more complicated than a can opener and a zip-top bag*
TIME: *30 minutes assembling the ingredients*
FEEDS: *6, pretty easily*

Summer Salad

FOR ME, LETTUCE does not define a salad. Particularly in the summer, when so many tasty vegetables are at their peak, I like to use them as the base, instead.

One of the most well known summer salads is the *Caprese*: basil, tomato, and mozzarella. When the tomatoes are ripe, there's nothing better, but I like to play around with it, sometimes adding slices of avocado, or changing the components to grape tomatoes, feta, and mint.

Another vegetable I like to use as a salad base is zucchini, as in my suggestion for zukes, almonds, and Parmesan, an idea I've borrowed from a New York restaurant called the Red Cat. You can sauté the zucchini with a bit of olive oil and lemon juice, and serve it at room temperature, tossed with the nuts and cheese.

If you must have lettuce, tweak the ratio and instead of having it be the focus of the salad, treat it as one of many ingredients. That's how I like my salad of avocado, Boston lettuce, and peas.

As for dressings, in the summer, lighter is better. A mixture of lemon juice and hazelnut oil, or a little sweet balsamic vinegar whisked with olive oil is all you need. Sometimes, I rub the inside of a salad bowl with a cut clove of garlic, then at the last second toss lettuce with a few dribbles of excellent olive oil. Of course, sea salt and freshly ground pepper are summer salad absolutes!

Three Summer Salads:

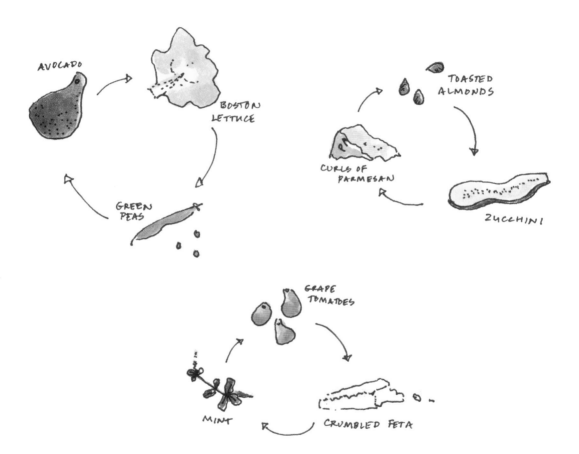

AVOCADO

BOSTON
LETTUCE

GREEN
PEAS

TOASTED
ALMONDS

CURLS OF
PARMESAN

ZUCCHINI

GRAPE
TOMATOES

MINT

CRUMBLED FETA

Apricot-Thyme Clafouti

It's a no-brainer that fruit desserts are best in season, but you can make this fruit-studded custard with high-quality canned apricots in light syrup any time of year. Just drain the apricots before you use them and reduce the sugar by one tablespoon. I prefer cooked apricots to raw ones, anyway. I think that, cooked, they lose a certain mealiness that always competes with their wonderful flavor.

2 tablespoons butter, plus extra for greasing the baking dish

4 tablespoons sugar, plus ½ cup

A few sprigs of fresh thyme

3 cups pitted and halved apricots

4 large eggs

1 cup milk

½ vanilla bean, halved lengthwise

½ cup all-purpose flour

pinch of salt

1. Grease a pie pan or ceramic baking dish and set aside.
2. Place a nonstick skillet (if you've got one) over high heat for a minute. Turn down the heat to medium-high and melt the butter. When the foam subsides, add the 4 tablespoons of sugar, the thyme, and the apricots. Let them sit there for a minute. Then carefully stir them with a spoon, or do the fancy chef trick of flipping the contents of your pan over with the flick of your wrist. Be careful—you don't want the apricots to fall apart. Depending on their ripeness, you'll be done after 3 to 5 minutes—the apricots should be a little softened and golden but not mushy. Set aside to cool.
3. Make the custard: In a bowl, beat together the eggs and remaining ½ cup of sugar with a whisk until frothy—a minute or so. Scrape the innards of the vanilla bean into the milk (you can toss the cleaned pod into your sugar bowl if you'd like to have vanilla sugar around). Add the milk to the egg mixture and mix until combined. Add the flour and salt—gradually, so it doesn't lump up too badly; give it a good whisk. Preheat oven to 375°F

4. In the greased pie pan or ceramic baking dish, strew the apricots and thyme in an even layer. Then pour the custard over them. Pop it into the oven—it'll take 25 to 35 minutes and will be done when it has puffed up a bit and is golden brown. Serve at room temperature. Yum!

SPECIAL EQUIPMENT: *A nonstick skillet and an ovenproof baking dish*
TIME: *1 hour*
FEEDS: *6 people who really like dessert*

∴ FRUIT ♥ HERBS ∾

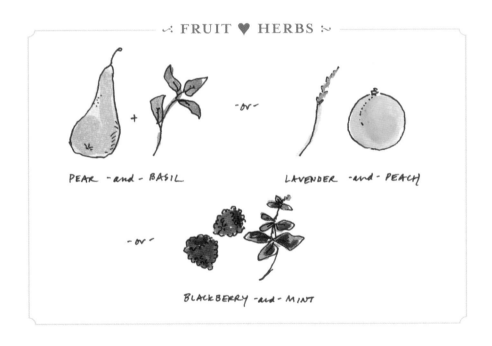

PEAR -and- BASIL

-or-

LAVENDER -and- PEACH

-or-

BLACKBERRY -and- MINT

4. Put a slice of toast in the bottom of a shallow soup bowl and ladle a generous helping of tomato on top, making sure to get lots of the lovely vinaigrette and tomato juices. Serve it up.

TIME: *10 to 15 minutes of working time, plus time to let the tomatoes marinate*
FEEDS: *6 as a first course*

◁ GETTING RID OF GARLIC SMELLS ◠

*T*HEY SELL FANCY bars of "soap" at gourmet shops to help you get rid of garlicky hands, but all you have to do is this: wash your hands under hot water with regular soap, all the while rubbing your fingertips on a stainless-steel utensil. It works.

Roasted Chicken with Watercress

A *lovely combination of chicken and greens. It might sound like a bad idea to roast a chicken in August, but I love the tomato-corn-chicken triumvirate that's best in high summer. What I do is roast the chicken earlier in the day, before the guests come, and serve it at room temperature, with the sauce just lightly reheated in a small pan on top of the stove. That way our tragically small air conditioner has had time to win the battle against our little furnace . . . I mean, oven.*

A very nice chicken, preferably free-range, 3 to 4 pounds

Kosher salt and pepper

1 onion, unpeeled and split in half

½ lemon

2 or 3 strips bacon

½ to ¾ cup water or white wine

A bunch of watercress, washed and dried

1. Preheat the oven to 425°F.
2. Rinse the ol' bird and pat her dry. Put her on a rack in the middle of a snug roasting pan. Salt and pepper the cavity, then put the neck, gizzard, and heart inside; discard the liver.
3. Wedge inside half of the onion and the lemon half. Drape the bacon over the breasts and the tops of the drumsticks. Salt and pepper the outside. Throw the other half of the onion in the bottom of the roasting pan, along with ¼ cup of water.
4. Get the bird in the oven. Wait! Don't walk away . . . you have work to do. Every 15 minutes you have to baste the bird—the bacon helps you, because it sort of bastes the chicken itself. But don't forget, or you'll be sorry!
5. A 3- to 4-pound bird will probably take 1½ hours to cook, but sometimes things go slower or faster, so the best way to check is to periodically stick a meat thermometer in at the junction of breast and thigh, taking the bird out when you hit 170°F. Just be careful not to have the tip of the thermometer resting on the bone, or you'll have an overly high temperature reading. If, toward the last half-hour of the cooking time, the bacon is looking petrified, take it off and let the bird brown beautifully.
6. Take the bird out of the oven. Lift it out of the roasting pan, draining the juices back into the pan, and put it on a platter tented with tinfoil for as long as you like. Personally, I like my roast chicken lukewarm. Meanwhile . . .

NOT ON LOVE ALONE

Green-market Eating

FOR ME, THE best part about cooking in the summertime is the Union Square Greenmarket's extravaganza of fruits and vegetables. In the spring or fall I often go to the market myself mid-morning, but in the summer I rouse JS with the promise of a real breakfast if he comes with me to the green market and carries the bags. (We also have a little collapsible shopping cart that is very desirable for this, the proof being that several old ladies have come up to us and complimented us upon it.)

The Union Square Greenmarket is just the hub of dozens of farmers' markets that dot the city from day to day. As the main one, it's open four days a week, with the largest markets on Friday and Saturday. It's always a bit hard for me to control myself in the market during the summer. I have to be very strict about the amount of money I'm willing to spend, or else I'll come home with a large selection of adorable, strange, and somewhat pricey rare fruits and vegetables. My heirloom-tomato budget, alone . . .

Farmers' market shopping is a valuable way to educate yourself about what fruit and vegetables are really supposed to smell, feel, look, and taste like. If you don't know where to find a farmers' market near you, try the USDA's Web site at www.ams.usda.gov. You can also check local magazines and newspapers for locations.

Ice Cream with Caramel and Toasted Almonds

There's no better, or easier, dessert in the summer than ice cream, since somebody else has made it for you. I do like to fuss about with toppings, however. Here's a good one.

1 handful raw almonds

1 cup sugar

¼ cup water

½ cup or more heavy cream

Squeeze of lemon juice

1 tablespoon unsalted butter

Store-bought vanilla ice cream

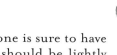

1. Toast the almonds at 350°F in your toaster oven (which someone is sure to have given you as a wedding present). When they're done—they should be lightly golden—give 'em a very rough chop. Set aside.
2. Put the sugar in a small, heavy-bottomed saucepan. Carefully pour ¼ cup of water on top. Run your finger though the sugar to make sure it's all been moistened. Turn the heat on to medium.
3. Don't touch the pan! Watch the sugar until it has all dissolved. *Then* you can give it a very gentle swirl. Cook it, swirling once or twice, until it is a nice dark amber color, 8 to 10 minutes. Be careful as you get to the end of the cooking time, as burnt sugar is not a joy to clean.
4. Off the heat, pour in the heavy cream and stir like you mean it. It'll boil furiously and look like a mistake for a few moments, but don't worry. When it's smooth, you can add a little more heavy cream to taste if the caramel is too strong for you. Add the lemon juice and the butter, and stir until the butter is melted. The caramel will thicken as it cools. Leave it on the counter until you need it, but it should be refrigerated overnight (and can stay in there for weeks for future ice cream adornments).
5. At dessert time, scoop out some vanilla ice cream and top with a spoonful or two (or three) of caramel and a sprinkle of chopped almonds. You could also add some raspberries if you'd like.

TIME: *10 minutes to make the sauce and toast the almonds*
FEEDS: *This recipe makes about 1 cup of sauce.*

NOT ON LOVE ALONE

SUMMER COCKTAIL PARTY

You've just been on your best behavior. . . now for your worst. The tidbits and hors d'oeuvres here are very simple, and can be scattered around the party on platters so guests can feed themselves. This is a true cocktail party, so there's not enough food here to sustain hours of drinking and talking—if guests stay too late, order a pizza. But there's plenty of food for fifteen people in a two- to three-hour window.

30 quail eggs

Celery salt

Sea salt

At my butcher shop, quail eggs come in flats of thirty. They're adorable, speckled things, and when you crack them, the inside of the shell is a delicate celadon green. Their flavor is chicken-eggy, but more delicate and a bit sweeter. All you need to do is set them in barely boiling water for 5 minutes, run them under the cold tap to cool them, and serve them in a bowl with a dish of sea salt and a dish of celery salt alongside. Sometimes I partially peel a few to encourage eaters, but at a recent party (and I think this tells you something about the sort of people JS and I spend time with) people were breaking the quail eggshells on their foreheads. Of course, that was *after* the keg stands . . .

Rubbed Toast

It's very hard to say just how much bread you might want here, because it depends on the size of the loaf. What I can tell you is that you want to cut it into bite-size wedges, each about the size of a tortilla chip, before you serve it; each wedge counts as a serving. Your goal here is about 40 servings.

Several ½-inch slices country bread

2 cloves garlic, halved

2 very ripe tomatoes

Olive oil

¼ lb. prosciutto, sliced very thin

10 anchovies cured in oil

Sea salt

1. Using your toaster, or a grill pan with ridges, toast or grill the bread until it's very dark but not burned. Immediately rub one side of the toast with a half clove of garlic.
2. Cut the tomatoes in half and rub the cut sides against the toast, really soaking the bread with the juices. Use each half-tomato until it's given all it can give, juice-wise, then move on to the next. Drizzle each slice with a hint of olive oil. Cut the toast into wedges. Sprinkle about twenty with sea salt. Lay a thin slice of prosciutto on ten others, giving it an attractive ripple when you cover the bread. Finally, garnish ten others with an anchovy curled up loosely in the center. Arrange the toasts casually on a platter and put it out for your guests to enjoy.

TIME: *15 minutes*

FEEDS: *This recipe makes 40 portions.*

NOT ON LOVE ALONE

Fried Squash Blossoms

I have a thing for these, but whether it's the idea of eating a blossom, or the whole fried batter—salt angle, I don't know. You shouldn't make these years ahead of time, but they drain very easily on a cookie rack on top of some paper towel, and are just as good at room temperature as they are warm. Just remember to salt them liberally.

20 zucchini or squash blossoms	1 cup seltzer water
Olive oil, for frying	Sea salt
1⅓ cup all-purpose flour	

1. Carefully rinse the blossoms and dry them on paper towels or a clean kitchen towel. They need to be as dry as you can get them.
2. Fill a large skillet ¼ inch up the side with olive oil, and turn the heat to medium. Roll out some paper towel and put a cookie rack over it.
3. While the oil's heating, make the batter, which is essentially paste: Sift the flour into a medium-size bowl, then, stirring constantly with a whisk, add the seltzer in a slow, steady stream until the batter has the consistency of sour cream or pancake batter.
4. Using a deft, light touch, hold each blossom by its stem end and give the flower a quick swirl in the batter. (It's a good idea to have the batter bowl right next to the stove.) Lay the flower in the hot oil (it might pop a bit, so be prepared to stand back). Continue with the other blossoms, stopping when the pan is full but each blossom has room to breathe. Turn the blossoms over with tongs as they become golden, then fish the finished blossoms out of the oil with the strainer or slotted spoon. Sprinkle them with salt. Let them rest on the cookie rack. Keep them at room temperature until you need them. These will go quickly.

SPECIAL EQUIPMENT: *A bamboo-handled strainer, the sort you can find at Chinese cooking-supply stores, is very useful here, but your average slotted spoon will do in a pinch.*
TIME: *30 minutes*
FEEDS: *This recipe makes 20 blossoms.*

Fennel and Tapenade on Toast

This was an hors d'oeuvre I started making after eating something similar at 'ino, a paninoteca on Bedford Street, a few blocks from our apartment. This little cubbyhole of a restaurant serves grilled panini, but also has a selection of excellent (and reasonably priced) bruschettas. Sometimes in a pinch before a dinner party, I send JS down there to get a plate full of them, which I then cut in half for hors d'oeuvres. Unconventional takeout, to be sure, but nobody complains!

A baguette, sliced very thinly on the bias, at least 25 slices

1 large, squat bulb of fennel, stalks and bottom trimmed

Juice of ½ lemon

3 tablespoons good olive oil

Sea salt and pepper

¼ cup tapenade (French black-olive spread) purchased at a gourmet shop, or ¼ cup finely chopped cured black Provençal olives

1. Preheat your oven to 250°F. Alternatively, use your toaster oven on the lowest setting. Lay the baguette slices out in a single layer on a cookie sheet and pop them in the oven. Let them toast for 30 minutes, until they're crispy like a cracker and slightly blond about the edges.
2. Meanwhile, cut the fennel bulb in half and slice it as thinly as you can on a mandoline. If the fennel is really fat and squat, you might have to cut it to quarters to achieve the ease of mandolining. You should have about 3 cups of tissue-thin fennel. Move the shaved fennel to a bowl and toss it with the lemon juice, olive oil, a pinch of sea salt, and some pepper. Set aside for 15 minutes to allow the flavors to commingle.
3. When the toasts have come out of the oven, let them cool, then top them with a tablespoon of the fennel and a small dab of the tapenade. Arrange them on a platter and serve.

SPECIAL EQUIPMENT: *A mandoline, which can be purchased in plastic for less than $20 and is invaluable for slicing fennel, potatoes, or apples paper thin*
TIME: *30 minutes*
FEEDS: *This makes about 25 toasts.*

NOT ON LOVE ALONE

Radishes with Butter and Salt

2 bunches of radishes
(you want about 35 radishes)

Slab of very good French butter, a bit soft

Small pile of sea salt

This is beyond easy and very tasty, the heat of the radishes tempered by the creaminess of the butter and made more flavorful by the sea salt. Some people (by which I mean, healthy people) like to dip their radishes in ice water and then into the salt, bypassing the butter. That produces a sharper, spicier flavor. All you need to do is clean and trim the radishes, and display them prettily alongside the butter and the salt on a platter. I always include a small knife or two to aid with the butter, though if it's very soft the radish can do all the work itself.

Tomatoes Stuffed with Feta and Chives

The most amazing thing about cocktail parties is that the thing that takes the longest to make is always the first to disappear down people's throats.

1 cup feta cheese, crumbled (goat's-milk feta is best)

¼ cup good olive oil

¼ cup snipped fresh chives

Freshly ground pepper

Kosher salt, to taste

1 pint cherry tomatoes

Fresh chive tips for decoration

1. First, make the filling: In a small bowl or a zip-top bag, combine the crumbled feta, the olive oil, and the snipped chives, along with a hearty helping of pepper. Taste for salt before you add any—feta can pack a pretty salty punch. Combine and set aside at room temperature.
2. Prep the tomatoes: Cut the tops off and discard them. Using a melon baller or teaspoon, hollow out the tomatoes, tossing the seeds. Then, slice a minuscule layer off the bottom of the cherry tomatoes, barely more than the skin, just enough to give the tomato a less precarious perch. Line them up on a plate.
3. Fill the suckers: Take a teaspoon and fill each tomato so there's a nice little mound above the rim. Top with a longer chive tip for that Martha Stewart touch. Repeat, repeat, repeat.

SPECIAL EQUIPMENT: *Get ready . . . I'm going to tell you to use a melon baller. Don't have one? For shame! Actually, neither do I. You can use a small teaspoon.*
TIME: *45 minutes*
FEEDS: *This recipe makes about 25 stuffed tomatoes.*

Not on Love Alone

Bellinis

Famously invented at Harry's Bar in Venice, a Bellini is a sweet-tart summertime drink that makes the best use of peaches this side of peach pie. You can make your own puree, as I do here, or you can be lazy and buy peach nectar, tarted up with some lemon juice.

½ lb. very ripe white peaches

Juice of ½ lemon

¼ cup water

A few teaspoons of sugar, to taste

Raspberries

A bottle of Prosecco (Italian sparkling wine) (See Champagne and Other Bubblies on page 42)

1. Loosen the peach skins by submerging the peaches in boiling water for 30 seconds, then running them under cold water. Peel the peaches (the skin should slip off easily), pit them, and cut them into hunks. Cover them with the lemon juice and water. Let them sit about 15 minutes.
2. Slide the peaches into the blender, and give them a whiz. Taste for sugar—it shouldn't be too tart, but we're not making piña coladas here. Elegantly fruity should be the goal. Pour the puree into a pitcher and refrigerate it.
3. To serve, drop a raspberry into the bottom of a champagne flute, then add a dollop of the peach puree. Fill the rest of the glass with Prosecco.

SPECIAL EQUIPMENT: *A blender*
TIME: *20 minutes*
QUENCHES: *Face it, if you have friends like ours, you need to double this recipe. Makes about 8 Bellinis.*

Quick Notes on Summertime Entertaining

𝒥HE BEST PART of summer entertaining is how easily it falls into your lap. There are cheap flowers everywhere, and everything that's delicious seems to be in season. You just have to collect it and present it to your guests.

- ℘ Watch the weather. If it's going to be ninety-five degrees, don't start the party at 6:00 PM. Part of the joy of a summer weekend is how late things can begin because of the late sunsets. Don't broil your guests but plan ahead and invite them for when things might be a little bit cooler.

- ℘ On that note, keep an ample supply of nonalcoholic drinks on hand, particularly sparkling water with some lemon. Dehydration is not pretty. Also, get an extra bag of ice.

- ℘ Alcohol, on the other hand, should be carefully considered. I would stick with a special drink (like the two I've given here), plus some white wine and bottled beer on ice. If you're doing this inside, and you have an all-white decorating scheme, skip red wine entirely.

The Last Gasp Menu

STUFFED ZUCCHINI WITH GOAT CHEESE (PAGE 158)
&
TOMATO RISOTTO (PAGE 160)
&
FAST PEACH TART (PAGE 162)

~

Three Basil Pastas

FUSILLI WITH ZUCCHINI, GARLIC, AND BASIL (PAGE 164)
&
FARFALLE WITH RICOTTA, LEMON, BASIL, AND PEAS (PAGE 165)
&
SPAGHETTI PESTO WITH CROUTONS (PAGE 166)

THE LAST GASP

~

Stuffed Zucchini with Goat Cheese

In France, they have these perfect little round courgettes that are excellent for stuffing. Here, just get the smallest, cutest zukes you can find. If you go for a regular-size squash, I personally think half a zucchini is enough, but eat up a whole one if you prefer (just double the recipe).

4 small (no less than 4 inches long) or 2 medium-size zucchini

2 tablespoons olive oil

2 medium onions, sliced very thin into half-moons

½ cup white wine

1 cake of the freshest goat cheese you can find (about ½ cup), crumbled

¼ cup chopped basil

2 tablespoons chopped mint

Kosher salt and pepper

1 tablespoon plain dried bread crumbs

1. Set up a steamer that can fit all of the whole zucchini at one time. Fill the bottom of the pot with at least 4 inches of water, cover, and bring to a boil. In the meantime, prep the zukes: If you're using the little squashes that look like mini pumpkins, cut the tops off, reserve, and then attack the innards of the zucchini with a teaspoon, hollowing the whole thing out without doing damage to the structural integrity of the vegetable. Keep the zucchini innards in a pile on your cutting board for later. For the smaller version of conventional zucchini, slice off the top quarter lengthwise and keep that as a lid; hollow out the rest. Normal-size zucchini should be cut in half lengthwise, and both sides hollowed out. Salt the cavities of your zucchini.

2. Get the suckers into the steamer, cut side down, including the caps. Close the lid, and let the zukes steam until the flesh can be comfortably pierced with the tip of a paring knife but they don't show any signs of collapse, about 5 minutes. They should still be the brightest green. Take them out of the steamer and set aside.

Not on Love Alone

3. Now for the filling: finely chop the reserved zucchini innards. Then, heat the olive oil in a large skillet over high heat until it shimmers. Add the sliced onion, season with salt, and give it a healthy sauté for 8 to 10 minutes. You want the onion to become a rich, tawny caramel color. At this point, add the chopped zucchini, another pinch of salt, and a generous amount of pepper, and stir to combine. Add the white wine, turn the heat down to medium-low, and let the wine boil off completely, about 4 to 6 minutes. Pour the contents of the pan into a large mixing bowl and set aside to cool.
4. Preheat the oven to 450°F.
5. When the filling is just a bit warm, fold in the crumbled goat cheese and the herbs. Test for seasoning—beware of adding too much salt, as the goat cheese can be quite salty. Arrange the zuke shells in a baking dish, fill each cavity generously, then sprinkle the tops with a light dusting of dried bread crumbs. Add another drizzle of olive oil. Perch the caps on top, then carefully slide them into the oven. Bake for 12 to 15 minutes, or until the bread crumbs have browned and the cheese is bubbling away. Serve hot.

SPECIAL EQUIPMENT: *An ovenproof ceramic baking dish; a colander or perforated insert for a pot for steaming*
TIME: *About 1 hour, including baking time*
FEEDS: *4*

Tomato Risotto

Risotto is hands-on all the way—the constant stirring keeps the rice from sticking and builds up the lovely starches that make it so creamy. There are some wonderful herbs in this risotto, but the most distinctive is the marjoram, which I suggest making the extra effort to find fresh. Just a small pinch will perfume the whole dish.

4 medium, very ripe tomatoes

5 cups chicken stock

3 tablespoons unsalted butter

1 tablespoon olive oil

½ small onion, chopped fine

1 very small clove garlic, minced

Sea salt and freshly ground black pepper

2 cups Arborio rice

Heaping ½ cup freshly grated Parmesan cheese

½ cup chopped fresh herbs, including basil, marjoram, and flat-leaf parsley

Shaved Parmesan cheese and torn basil leaves, for garnish

1. Peel the tomatoes: bring a pot of water to a boil. Drop the tomatoes in, one by one, for about 30 seconds. Run these under cold water, cut an X-shaped incision into the skin, and pull the skin off. Then, seed and dice them.
2. Pour the stock into a pot and heat to the simmer.
3. In a medium-size heavy-bottomed saucepan, melt 2 tablespoons of the butter with the 1 tablespoon of olive oil. When the foam subsides, add the onion and garlic, and cook over medium heat until translucent, a few minutes. Add the tomatoes, a pinch of salt and grinding of pepper, give a stir, and turn the heat down to low. Cook, stirring occasionally, for 10 minutes—you want the tomatoes to break down, but not completely.
4. Add the Arborio rice to the tomato mixture and stir to coat with a wooden spoon. Turn the heat up to medium, or even medium-high—risotto needs a lively flame and should never be soupy. Starting with ½ cup and then additional ¼ cups, add the simmering broth to the rice, stirring all the while. Once the liquid has evaporated, you can add some more. After about 15 minutes taste a few grains. You don't want mushy rice; it should still be slightly firm (but not crunchy!).

5. When you estimate you have about 5 minutes left to go, add the remaining table-spoon of butter, the Parmesan cheese, and the chopped herbs. Turn down the heat to low and continue adding the stock. You should now have that wonderful creamy risotto consistency, with the rice tinted pink from the tomatoes. Taste for salt and adjust as necessary. Garnish with shaved Parmesan cheese and torn basil leaves, and serve.

TIME: *35 minutes*
FEEDS: *4, generously*

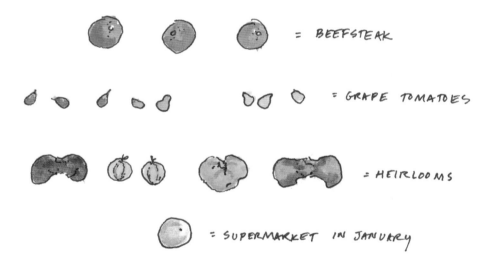

Fast Peach Tart

The hardest part of this tart is peeling the peaches, which you can do the same way you peel toma-toes, in boiling water—leave them in for a full minute. So it ain't very hard at all, actually . . .

A sheet of prepared puff pastry from the freezer section, defrosted

3 tablespoons butter

6 ripe peaches

4 tablespoons sugar

1. Preheat the oven to 425°F.
2. Make sure the puff pastry is completely thawed. Unfold the sheet onto a nonstick cookie sheet that's been greased with a tiny bit of butter. If you don't have a non-stick sheet, use a cookie sheet lined with parchment paper that's been greased with a bit of butter. Prick the center of the puff pastry with a fork a few times. Stick it in the fridge.
3. Microwave the butter so it melts (or melt it in a small pan on the stove).
4. Slice the peaches by cutting the fruit in half to stone it, then slicing each half into ¼-inch-thick half-moons rather than into wedges, as you might for a pie— the uniform thickness is important here. Then, starting at the top of the puff pastry, and leaving about a ½-inch edge, arrange the slices, nicely overlapping, in whatever attractive pattern you feel like. Brush the fruit with the melted but-ter, and sprinkle with the sugar.
5. Put the tart in the oven and immediately turn the oven heat down to 375°F. Bake for 20 to 25 minutes, checking occasionally to poke down any renegade bubbles of pastry that might be forming at the center. Bake until the crust is quite golden brown and the peaches have caramelized a little. Be brave—you don't want car-bon, but the flavor and texture are best when it's thoroughly cooked.

SPECIAL EQUIPMENT: *Parchment paper comes in handy here. You can find it in the supermarket aisle, with the tinfoil and the trash bags.*
TIME: *About 45 minutes total, but only about 15 minutes active time*
FEEDS: *10, easily. This is also great for breakfast the next day.*

Other fruits that work on this tart:

NOT ON LOVE ALONE

show you how to do this before you attempt it on your own, but it's fun). When they're nicely toasted on one or two sides, slide them out onto some waiting paper towels, which will absorb the excess oil.

4. By this point, your spaghetti will be perfectly cooked. Drain it and add it to the pesto in the serving bowl, tossing it like a salad to evenly distribute. Add the croutons and toss again. Serve piping hot with more Parmesan cheese on the side. After you're done eating, try not to breathe on your neighbor.

NOTE: *To toast the pine nuts, place them in a dry pan over medium-low heat, stirring occasionally, until they are fragrant and golden brown.*

SPECIAL EQUIPMENT: *A blender or food processor is de rigueur.*
TIME: *Almost none at all for the pesto; altogether, as long as it takes the pasta to cook, about 8 minutes, plus a few minutes for prep and boiling water*
FEEDS: *4*

Fromage!

a Cheese Play in Five Acts

ACT FOUR: *The Hard Italians*

SCENE: *Again, the holy temple of Bleecker Street cheese, Murray's Cheese Shop. J stands before a large bin of cheese wedges, propped on top of a large wheel of Parmesan. JS stands by patiently.*

J, *confused*. Maybe I should get this one? (*She holds up a hefty wedge of Parmigiano Reggiano.*) Is this too much cheese?

JS, *looking at J as if she's crazy*. How's it different from this one here? (*He squints to read the label.*) It's organic Parmigiano Reggiano. It's rarer.

J. And more expensive. (*She sighs.*) Maybe I'll just get some Pecorino Romano for the tang. And some regular Parmesan.

JS. Is that enough? (*He starts to peer into the refrigerated case.*) I think we should get some other cheeses, as long as we're here . . .

(*black out*)

NOT ON LOVE ALONE

OCTOBER

Rabbit Stew vs. Rabbit Food

Rabbit Stew vs. Rabbit Food

JS WAS A little apprehensive the first time he ate rabbit, but after one bite the Easter bunny was forgotten forever. Rabbit is flavorful, leaner than chicken, and creates a spot of interest in an otherwise dreary sea of chicken cutlets and turkey burgers. It does well with bold accompaniments, as in the recipe I've included here, which is a tribute to a dish we had at our friend Ronny's house.

And while some people, like Ronny, feed us rabbit, we feed others vegetarian feasts. Our friend Kristin is a vegan with a capital V. Actually, you can just capitalize all those letters with Kristin. So JS dared me to make a vegan meal, and while I didn't delve into the mysterious world of tempeh and protein powders, I did a credible (if not totally nutritionally balanced) job. The second menu is merely vegetarian, not vegan, but I suggest some radical alterations if you, too, want to go all the way.

Ronny's Rabbit Tribute

RABBIT AND TOMATO STEW (PAGE 172)

&

LES CRÊPES CÉLÈBRE DE MÈRE BLANC (PAGE 176)

&

BAKED PEARS WITH BROWN SUGAR (PAGE 178)

⁓

Rabbit Food

FALL VEGETABLES WITH HOLLANDAISE SAUCE (PAGE 180)

&

ORECCHIETTE WITH LENTILS, BUTTERNUT SQUASH,
AND CREAM (PAGE 182)

&

SAUTÉED APPLES WITH VANILLA (PAGE 185)

RONNY'S RABBIT TRIBUTE

Rabbit and Tomato Stew

Our friends Ronny and Isabelle are avid and excellent home cooks. While they can both whip up a mean meal, they don't play well together in the kitchen. I guess I should say that Ronny doesn't play well with Isabelle in the kitchen. When he's cooking, he's a rock, an island, a gladiator locked in a one-on-one battle with his stove. Meanwhile, Isabelle rolls her eyes.

One time, Ronny came up with a terrific braised-rabbit recipe, and had us guess the ingredients. I picked up the cinnamon, and Ronny helpfully pointed out the brightness of the orange. When I begged him for the recipe, he shrugged his shoulders and said he had made it up. So this is my made-up version of Ronny's made-up recipe, a tribute to the original lost to history.

1 rabbit, cut up into serving pieces (ask your butcher—he might need to order this for you, or already have it frozen on hand; just ask him to cut it up for you)

3 tablespoons all-purpose flour

Kosher salt and pepper

2 tablespoons olive oil

2 cloves garlic

1 large yellow onion, chopped

1 stalk celery, minced

1 medium carrot, peeled and cut into thin rounds

1 sprig of fresh thyme

1 cinnamon stick, broken in half

2 cups canned whole plum tomatoes, with their juice

Zest of ½ orange

4 tablespoons freshly squeezed orange juice—less than ½ orange

Handful of chopped fresh flat-leaf parsley

1. Rinse off the rabbit and pat it dry with paper towels.
2. Put the flour on a plate and season it with some salt and pepper. Heat the olive oil over a medium flame in the bottom of the cast-iron casserole. When the oil is hot, brown the rabbit: Roll it in the flour piece by piece, knocking off any

excess, and lay it gently in the pot. Don't crowd the pan—plan on doing at least two batches. Sear the rabbit on both sides, about 4 minutes a side. Regulate the heat to keep the flour from burning. Reserve the browned rabbit on a platter.

3. When the rabbit's browned, add the garlic and onion to the pot. Stir until you can smell the garlic, then add a good pinch of salt. Sauté, stirring for a few minutes, until the onion has gone translucent. Add the celery and the carrot. Stir around, cooking until there's good color on the vegetables, about 10 minutes.

4. At this point, add the thyme and the cinnamon stick. Let them swirl in the fat, then add the rabbit back into the pot and top with the 2 cups of plum tomatoes. (I always cut up the tomatoes on their way into the pot by using my kitchen scissors.) Give the contents of the pot a stir, look for a few heat bubbles, then cover the casserole tightly and turn down the heat to a minimum. Go do something else for a while.

5. Occasionally, you can stir things in the pot, just to make sure it's not cooking too fast, and to make sure nothing is sticking. But it should braise, almost undisturbed, for 2½ hours. At that point, take off the lid and inspect your stew. Beautiful, no? The cinnamon makes it smell terrific. Now, add the orange zest and the bit of orange juice that you reserved. Stir it around, then cover again and continue cooking for 30 minutes.

6. The rabbit should be done then, so tender that it's almost falling off the bones. Taste for salt and pepper. You can serve it right away with a sprinkling of parsley, or you can let it stand and gently reheat it before serving.

SPECIAL EQUIPMENT: *Just a large casserole, such as a Le Creuset*
TIME: *More than 3 hours, mostly unattended*
FEEDS: *4 to 6*

Rabbit and Game

My BUTCHER SHOP, Ottomanelli's, specializes in game, so no matter what fancy strikes me, they probably have it in the back, just waiting for me. A rabbit is child's play. Pheasant? Not a problem. Quail? Of course. For a while, they would tease me by asking if I needed any squab today, as I was deep into a Moroccan pigeon pie phase and seemed to be buying some every week. They even have some elk jerky on their stainless-steel counter, waiting for the day when somebody wants to eat elk jerky.

If you don't live down the block from Ottomanelli's, your game whims might have to wait for delivery from specialized butchers elsewhere. But don't you want to try cooking venison, at least once? Of course, I recommend buying any mail-order game from Ottomanelli's, at www.ottomanellimeats.com.

Sometimes game comes from actual game hunters. A friend of ours named CD, a sensitive, quiet soul and doctoral candidate in art history (perhaps we should call him Dr. CD), is also from Texas, wears cowboy boots, and goes pheasant hunting. One time he sent over a brace of pheasants for me to cook for a dinner party. The preparation involved a pair of needle-nosed pliers and a small knife to remove the shot. I had a great time.

QUAIL

SQUAB

VENISON LOIN

What Is Mirepoix?

BEFORE SITTING DOWN to write this book, I knew what mirepoix was, but I had no idea what its origin was. It's French, and for some reason I thought the name had something to do with peas (because *pois* is the French word for peas). It made a sort of convoluted sense because you dice the components of mirepoix, perhaps into pea-size pieces. Voilà!

However, I was tragically wrong. Mirepoix, according to the *Larousse Gastronomique*, is named after Monsieur Mirepoix, who was the first one to come up with the standard proportions of 2 parts onion to 1 part carrot and 1 part celery. Thousands of dishes start off this way, so Monsieur Mirepoix was on to something.

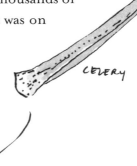

ONION

CELERY

CARROT

Les Crêpes Célèbre de Mère Blanc

This is a venerable French recipe, a potato cake from the wise and all-knowing Mother White. Who was Mother White, you ask? Beats me. But try these crepes, and I think you'll agree that Mother White, whoever she was, knew what she was doing.

These can also be served for dessert, if you want to dust them with sugar and put them under a fruit compote, or serve them with some other sweet thing.

1 lb. starchy potatoes, such as russets	1½ teaspoons kosher salt
4 egg whites	3 tablespoons heavy cream or crème fraîche
4 tablespoons all-purpose flour	
3 whole eggs	Clarified butter, for cooking (see note)

1. Peel the potatoes, cut them into large, uniform chunks, and put them in a pot with cold water. Bring the water to a boil and cook the spuds until they're tender, about 15 minutes. Drain, then immediately puree the potatoes into a large mixing bowl, using either a potato ricer (to work out your forearms) or a food mill (for your biceps). Let the potatoes cool for a minute or two.

2. In the meantime, in a smaller bowl, whisk the egg whites just until the albumen is broken up a little bit.

3. Back to the potatoes: Mix in the flour with a wooden spoon, then the whole eggs, one at a time. This will be looking decidedly gloopy. Then, add the egg whites in dribs and drabs, until all the eggs are finally incorporated. Throw in the salt and the bit of cream. The mixture should have the consistency of vanilla pudding.

4. Heat a large skillet or griddle over lively heat, and pour on a few teaspoons of clarified butter (watch out, it might spatter). Drop the potato mixture by soup-spoonfuls into the hot pan. The little crepes will spread and form all by themselves. Give them a minute or two to brown on one side, then flip them and brown on the other. They'll be the shape and color of silver-dollar pancakes. You can drain them on paper towels while you continue cooking, adding more clarified butter as necessary. I always like to make some deliberate "mistakes" so I, as the chef, will be forced to eat one. Or two. Try not to eat all the crepes before your guests arrive!

NOT ON LOVE ALONE

NOTE: *These crepes need to be cooked in clarified butter, which is easy to make. Simply melt a stick of butter in the top of a double boiler, then spoon off the milk solids that float to the top, pour off the clear, yellow butter, and discard the impurities that have sunk to the bottom. Unused clarified butter will keep in the fridge for a couple of weeks.*

SPECIAL EQUIPMENT: *A potato ricer or a food mill, to puree the potatoes and remove any lumps. (A food processor is vehemently not recommended—it makes potatoes gummy.) A roomy frying pan, or even a griddle, for ease of flipping, would also be nice.*
TIME: *About 1 hour, but you can make them ahead and reheat them in a low oven at serving time.*
FEEDS: *If you estimate 5 pancakes per person, about 6.*

∽ A MAN'S UTENSIL ∾

The Potato Ricer

ONCE, FOR CHRISTMAS, my cousin Patty gave JS an unusual gift. It was a potato ricer. Understandably confused, JS held it in the air for a moment, blinking, and said a perplexed thank-you. But Patty clarified. She told him that all good Irish households had a potato ricer, for making smooth mashed potatoes, and that it was the man's job to deal with the grunt work of squeezing the boiled potatoes through the ricer's tiny holes. JS is not one to shirk his responsibility. I should note that this remains JS's only active cooking duty to date.

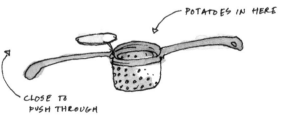

POTATOES IN HERE

CLOSE TO PUSH THROUGH

Baked Pears with Brown Sugar

This is a perfect fall dessert—and you can feel virtuous for eating fruit.

4 Bosc pears, peeled

2 tablespoons unsalted butter

4 tablespoons brown sugar

A drizzle of maple syrup
(the real sort, please)

1. Preheat the oven to 350°F.
2. Core the pears: attacking them from the bottom with a teaspoon, scoop out all the seeds and the fibrous heart of the pears, trying not to pierce the pear anywhere but the bottom as you do so. This takes a few minutes.
3. Have a rimmed baking sheet or little roasting pan ready. Take a pear, put ½ tablespoon of butter and 1 full tablespoon of brown sugar in the cavity, and stand it up on its end on the baking sheet. Do this with its friends. Once the pears are ready to go, drizzle the tops with some maple syrup and add a few drops of water to the bottom of the pan to keep the sugar from burning.
4. Bake for 25 to 30 minutes, depending on the ripeness of the pears (less time for riper pears), until the pears are soft, and the sugar is nice and runny. You can serve these right out of the oven, or just warm, and you can add some whipped cream if you're feeling decadent.

TIME: *30 minutes*
FEEDS: *4, but this is easily halved (or multiplied)*

✌ TARTING UP BAKED FRUIT ✌

*N*O BAKED FRUIT need remain unstuffed! Anything you want can go in the cavity for a bit of a dessert surprise. Chopped toasted pecans, golden raisins, a bit of chopped, candied ginger, or semisweet chocolate chips all add a bit of fun to the brown sugar and butter filling.

NOT ON LOVE ALONE

RABBIT FOOD

OF COURSE, THERE are those who won't eat rabbit stew, or any-thing else containing something that once walked on the earth. Some of these people are dear friends, and we call them vegetarians.

I embrace a good vegetarian meal, though I'm less happy with a vegan one, so the menu below is really vegetarian—for those who will eat cheese and eggs. But the hollandaise could easily be replaced by a robust vinaigrette, and you can serve the pasta without any cheese, or with cheese on the side for those who want it. I wouldn't tweak the sautéed apples, because the butter is irreplaceable, but you can ask the vegan guest of honor to bring along some sorbet for everyone.

Fall Vegetables with Hollandaise Sauce

The idea here is to gather as many colors, textures, and flavors you can get on one platter, then arrange them like a Dutch still life, with the sauce on the side.

FOR THE VEGETABLES:

3 red beets, trimmed

5 small golden beets, trimmed

1 pint Brussels sprouts

1 bulb fennel

1 bunch broccoli rabe

½ head cauliflower

1 bunch scallions

¼ lb. purple Peruvian potatoes

1 half-pint red pearl onions

2 tender hearts of celery, with leaves

½ cup vegetable stock, more as needed

2 stemmed portobello mushrooms

Olive oil as needed

Sea salt

FOR THE HOLLANDAISE:

3 egg yolks

1 teaspoon fresh lemon juice, or to taste

Sea salt and black pepper

1 stick unsalted butter, melted and kept hot

1. The beets, Brussels sprouts, and fennel should be steamed. (You should probably steam the beets in a large pot and do the Brussels sprouts and fennel in batches in a separate pot.) Prepare the vegetables as follows:

   Beets: Steam large beets for up to 40 minutes; smaller beets from 20 to 30 minutes. They're done when a knife tip slides in easily, as into a potato. Peel the cooked beets with a vegetable peeler or paring knife and cut them into thick wedges for serving.

   Brussels Sprouts: Keep the sprouts whole and cut an X into the bottom of each one with a paring knife. Steam them for about 10 minutes, so they're a bit tender but still retain their bright color. Run them under cold water to stop the cooking.

   Fennel: Trim off most of the fronds and tops of the bulb, cut the bulb into sixths, and trim the core. Drizzle with a tiny bit of olive oil, then steam for 10 to 12 minutes, until the outer layers become tender and a bit translucent.

Not on Love Alone

2. The broccoli rabe, cauliflower, scallions, onions, and purple potatoes can be boiled, in batches, in the same pot. Place a large pot of salted water to boil over high heat, and prepare the vegetables as follows:

Broccoli Rabe: Drop the broccoli rabe, bottom stems trimmed, into the rapidly boiling salted water for 2 to 4 minutes, then run it under cold water to stop the cooking.
Cauliflower: Trim the cauliflower into medium-large dramatic florets. Cook the florets in the boiling water for 5 to 7 minutes, then run them under cold water to stop the cooking. You want them to be tender, with a bit of resistance.
Scallions: Trim the ends, then blanch the scallions for two minutes in the boiling water. Drain, and rinse under cold water.
Purple Potatoes: Boil them whole in their skins, in salted water, about 10 minutes (or longer for larger ones). Let cool, then peel and slice into wedges.
Pearl Onions: While the potatoes are cooling, drop unpeeled pearl onions into the boiling water for 8 to 10 minutes. Cool them with cold water, slice off the root end, and squeeze to peel.

3. Cut the hearts of celery in half lengthwise down the middle, and lay them flat in a skillet. Add ½ cup vegetable stock, bring to a simmer, put the lid on slightly ajar, and cook for 10 minutes, or until the bottom of the celery is easily pierced with a knife.

4. Brush the mushrooms lightly with olive oil and lightly sauté them in a nonstick pan, about 3 minutes a side.

5. Arrange the vegetables on a platter and, right before serving, make the hollandaise: Blend together the egg yolks, lemon juice, and good pinches of salt and pepper. Then, keeping the machine running, pour the hot butter through the pour spout on the top in a very thin stream, stretching it out for about a minute. The hollandaise should be thickened at the end of a minute. Taste for seasoning and lemon, then pour into a serving bowl.

SPECIAL EQUIPMENT: *A food processor or hand blender*
TIME: *About 2 hours*
FEEDS: *This feast serves 6 to 8 as a hearty first course or main course.*

Orecchiette with Lentils, Butternut Squash, and Cream

This is a slightly unusual dish, but the earthiness of the lentils and the freshness of the squash really play well off one another. The bread crumbs add another textural element without much effort.

2 tablespoons unsalted butter

½ cup dried plain bread crumbs

Kosher salt

2 tablespoons olive oil

⅓ cup red onion or shallot, diced fine

2 cloves garlic, minced

¼ cup finely diced carrot

¼ cup finely diced celery

pinch of ground cumin

1 sprig of fresh thyme

⅓ cup dried Le Puy lentils (you can substitute brown lentils in a pinch)

1½ cup vegetable stock (or chicken stock)

1 lb. dried orecchiette pasta

1 cup peeled and diced butternut squash (pieces should be ¼ inch)

Black pepper, to taste

Pinch of hot pepper flakes (optional)

5 tablespoons heavy cream

Parmesan cheese for grating over the top

1. In a small frying pan, melt 1 tablespoon of the butter and, when the foam has subsided, add the bread crumbs. Toast over medium heat for a minute or two; set aside.
2. Put a pot of water on to boil for the pasta. Add a palmful of kosher salt. While the water is coming up to temperature, prepare the vegetables and heat a large frying pan on the stove. Add the olive oil, heat for a moment, then add the red onion and garlic. Add a pinch of kosher salt. Sauté until the red onion relaxes and starts to become translucent, about 3 minutes. Then, add the carrot and celery, sautéing well for at least 5 minutes more.
3. At this point, add the cumin and thyme to the pan and stir to combine. Then add the lentils, swirling them around so they're covered in the oil. Add the 1½ cups of stock (you could also substitute 1½ cups of water), bring to the boil, and then lower the heat to a minimum. The lentils will take about 12 minutes to cook.

NOT ON LOVE ALONE

November

Home for the Holidays

Home for the Holidays

IRPLANE FOOD IS typically some of the most repulsive in the world. The haute cuisine of the friendly skies is only the worst offender; the microwaved "sandwiches" in the Amtrak Northeast Corridor bar cars manage to be both slimy and dry at the same time; and the anemic burgers at the Arby's in rest stops along the New Jersey Turnpike are only good for a bad case of heartburn around about Baltimore. I know this, for I have eaten them all.

But, a few years ago, I was introduced to travel food done right. JS and I went to Japan for three weeks so he could watch the World Cup and I could eat all the Japanese food I could, all day long. One of the most amusing foodie delights was the cornucopia of bento boxes to be purchased at train stations (or from a food cart on the train itself). Ranging in price and variety, filled with sushi, seaweed salads, or noodles, these clever lunch boxes were chicer and better tasting than anything on this side of the Pacific. I had to have one on every train ride, hungry or not.

So, I've faked up a bento box in time for the Thanksgiving holidays, for when every newly married couple is making its way to his parents or hers. Believe me when I tell you you'll feel much better after eating this than you would that tragic hot dog that's been rotating under the heat lamp for two hours.

On the other end, I've included some light, quick soups to make—nary a turkey scrap in sight—when you're back home repenting your gluttonous ways. They're soothing and delicious, perfect for lifting your turkey stupor.

NOT ON LOVE ALONE

For the Plane, Train, or Automobile

FRITTATA WRAP (PAGE 190)

&

EDAMAME (PAGE 192)

&

FENNEL AND RADISH SALAD (PAGE 193)

&

SOMETHING EXTRA: CARROT SOUFFLÉ (PAGE 195)

⁓

Thanksgiving Detox

EGG DROP SOUP WITH MINT (PAGE 197)

&

CAULIFLOWER SOUP WITH CUMIN SEEDS AND PARSLEY (PAGE 198)

&

CHICKEN SOUP WITH GINGER, BARLEY, AND CHESTNUTS (PAGE 199)

FOR THE PLANE, TRAIN, OR AUTOMOBILE

Frittata Wrap

This is a take on a sushi roll, using tortilla wraps (or lavash, as you prefer), but you could always be more conventional and sandwich the frittata between layers of ciabatta or even a crusty baguette.

1 cup cooked sushi rice (prepared according to package directions and cooled)

2 teaspoons rice wine or white wine vinegar

1 scallion, sliced thinly on the bias, white and light green parts only

2 teaspoons sesame seeds

4 eggs, lightly beaten

½ teaspoon kosher salt

1½ teaspoons sugar

2 teaspoons unsalted butter

2 whole-wheat or spinach sandwich wraps

4 tablespoons softened cream cheese

4 ounces smoked salmon, thinly sliced

1. In a medium-size mixing bowl, combine the rice with the rice wine vinegar, then mix in the scallion and sesame seeds. You can do this with your hands, but that rice is awfully sticky.
2. Add the eggs, salt, and sugar, and mix to combine.
3. Heat a nonstick pan over medium heat, melt the butter, and swirl it about to cover the whole bottom. Pour in the egg mixture, making sure it's distributed evenly, then cover the pan and turn the heat down to medium low. Let the frittata cook, undisturbed, for 10 minutes.
4. After 10 minutes, check the eggs. The omelet should be completely firm on top and golden along the edges. Turn off the heat, and then upend the frittata onto a cutting board and let cool.
5. When the frittata is cool, cut it into inch-wide long strips. Take a sandwich wrap and spread it with a thin layer of cream cheese. (Scallion cream cheese would also

be good here, or, if you don't want to use the smoked salmon, a cream cheese with olives. Or you could nix the cream cheese altogether and use a smooth hummus. That could have olives, too. You get the picture.) Top with a few thin slices of salmon in a single layer.

6. Finish assembling the sandwich: Layer some strips of the frittata in a square in the center of the sandwich wrap, making sure to leave enough wrap free to fold up and roll the sandwich. Then, with the strips facing you horizontally, fold up the near edge of the bread over the frittata, fold the sides in, and roll up. The goal here is to wrap it like a burrito—a simple process, only somewhat convoluted when put into words.

7. Cut the sandwich in half, line the halves up next to each other, and wrap tightly in plastic wrap. Repeat steps 5 through 7 for the second sandwich. Keep in the fridge until you're ready to go.

SPECIAL EQUIPMENT: *A nonstick omelet pan is essential here.*
TIME: *About 20 minutes, not including time to cook the rice*
FEEDS: *2 hungry travelers*

⌇ SHOPPING FROM THE NEWSSTAND ∾

THIS IS WHAT you should buy instead of that cylinder of Sour Cream & Onion Pringles:

Cashew nuts
Pistachios
Dried apricots
Trail mix
Peanut M&M's

Edamame

These fresh soybeans, aka Japanese beer nuts, are widely available in the freezer section now, and they're ridiculously easy to make. Just bring some salted water to a boil and add the frozen edamame. After the water has come back to the boil, cook the edamame for three minutes, drain them, run them under cool water, and then shell them. Sprinkle them generously with salt, and keep in the refrigerator until you're ready to head out.

❧ OTHER BENTO BOXERS ❧

Roasted, salted pumpkin seeds
Home-popped popcorn
Cherry tomatoes
Wasabi peas
Smoked almonds
Japanese rice crackers

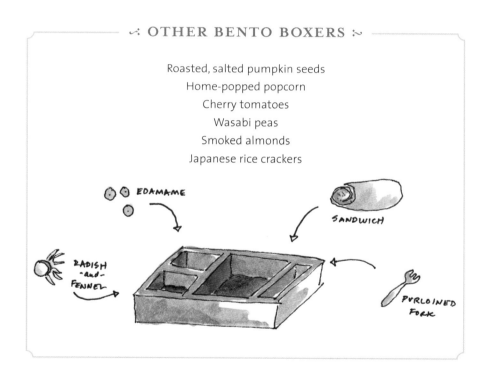

EDAMAME

SANDWICH

RADISH -and- FENNEL

PURLOINED FORK

NOT ON LOVE ALONE

Fennel and Radish Salad

This is refreshing and very easy to make. Just store the salad in a disposable plastic container and bring along a plastic fork (or procure one from the Amtrak bar car).

1 small bulb fennel	A drizzle of good olive oil
5 or 6 radishes	Sea salt and pepper
A squeeze of fresh lemon juice, to taste (about ½ lemon)	

Trim, wash, and dry the fennel, and trim and wash the radishes. Cut the fennel in half and run each half through the mandoline. Do the same with the radishes. Put both into a plastic container with a lid, add the lemon juice and olive oil, and salt and pepper to taste. Mix, and stick in the fridge until it's time to leave.

SPECIAL EQUIPMENT: *This salad is this salad because of a mandoline. The plastic varieties are cheap and endlessly useful.*
TIME: *2 minutes, if you're slow*
FEEDS: *2*

Something Extra

$\mathcal{A}$ WORD TO the wise. It pays to arrive for any holiday at your in-laws' house well-armed with a recipe you can prepare for the assembled masses. This carrot soufflé is particularly good because it requires so little time in the kitchen, and yet you can do so much with it. That way, you're helpful and thoughtful, but you don't get in the way while your mother-in-law roasts the turkey or worries about the stuffing.

The best part is that the soufflé looks sophisticated and impressive, but is a snap to make. Plus, if you anticipate that the kitchen on Turkey Day afternoon will closely resemble O'Hare International Airport, you can make the soufflé in the morning and reheat it in the already hot oven for about ten minutes just before serving.

Carrot Soufflé

This is a Carry family tradition that originally came from our erstwhile upstairs neighbor, Betsy Newell.

3 slices white bread	3 eggs, beaten
1 cup milk	4 tablespoons grated Swiss cheese
7 carrots, boiled until tender	1 teaspoon kosher salt
2 tablespoons unsalted butter, melted	5 teaspoons sugar

1. Preheat the oven to 350°F.
2. Put the bread in a small bowl and cover with the milk. Let it soak for 5 minutes, until the bread has wicked up all the liquid.
3. Place the bread and the remaining ingredients in the bowl of a food processor. Blend them until you have a bright orange, uniform batter. An easy way to impress the in-laws, no?
4. Put the mixture into a greased soufflé dish. Prepare a bain-marie (see note), which will keep the bottom of your soufflé from scorching.
5. Bake the soufflé for 1 hour 10 minutes to 1 hour 15 minutes, or until the top is puffed and lightly golden. Serve piping hot.

NOTE: *To set up a bain-marie, boil some water in a kettle, put the soufflé dish (or other ceramic baking dish) in a roasting pan on the oven rack, and then pour the boiling water at least ½ inch up the sides of the soufflé dish. Then simply slide the rack back in the oven. (Trying to do this on the counter before transferring it to the oven is a great way to get scalded.)*

SPECIAL EQUIPMENT: *A blender or food processor*
TIME: *About 1½ hours total, but much of that is unattended baking time.*
FEEDS: *Everyone at the Thanksgiving table*

THANKSGIVING DETOX

After the week o' turkey, it's time to turn over a new leaf, culinarily speaking. However, the turkey has made you so tired you can barely turn on the stove, never mind run out to the store and buy anything for dinner. Despite that, the mere idea of vats of grease delivered to your door courtesy of your local Chinese takeout makes you shudder.

My solution? Easy soups made from ingredients that are mostly on hand, or easily purchased before you leave for vacation.

Here is my own ersatz brand of Chinese-homeopathy-cum-old-wives'-tales of what makes you feel better when you eat it. Some of the ingredients—mint, cumin, ginger, star anise—clear your head and settle your stomach. So you're not only eating something yummy, you're eating something that's good for you. How great is that?

NOT ON LOVE ALONE

Egg Drop Soup with Mint

There's nothing simpler than this soup. With only four ingredients, it couldn't be faster or easier. My one whole-hearted recommendation is that you use real homemade chicken stock, which, I hope, is lurking in your freezer at this very moment. The taste of this soup is so pure that homemade stock really completes it. If homemade chicken stock is not in the cards, choose a low-sodium chicken stock, preferably one in a laminated box rather than a can—I think the canned variety develops a metallic tang as it sits on the shelf.

4 cups homemade chicken stock

2 eggs, lightly beaten

1½ teaspoons kosher salt (if using homemade stock, which is unsalted; if not,
just add sea salt to taste at the end)

1 tablespoon chopped fresh mint

Sea salt

1. Bring the 4 cups of stock to a low boil in a medium-size saucepan. If using homemade stock, add the kosher salt. Turn down the heat to medium-low.
2. Pour the beaten eggs into the pot in a slow stream, whisking the entire time. The eggs will set up immediately, forming lacy webs in the soup. Turn off the heat.
3. Add the mint and the sea salt to taste. Pour into bowls and eat.

TIME: *5 minutes*
FEEDS: *2 people in need of revivification*

Cauliflower Soup with Cumin Seeds and Parsley

Only slightly more complicated than the previous recipe, the trickiest part of this recipe is smashing the cooked cauliflower against the side of the pot with a wooden spoon.

1 teaspoon whole cumin seeds

2 teaspoons olive oil

1 shallot, minced

3 cups small cauliflower florets—less than a head of cauliflower

4 cups homemade chicken stock (boxed low-sodium stock can be substituted)

1½ teaspoons kosher salt (if using homemade stock, which is unsalted; if using boxed broth, taste for salt first)

1 tablespoon unsalted butter (optional)

2 tablespoons finely chopped flat-leaf parsley

Sea salt and pepper to taste

1. In a small frying pan, toast the cumin seeds over medium heat until they're fragrant. Spill them out onto the counter and bruise them slightly with the bottom of a glass or the side of a chef's knife.
2. Heat the oil over medium heat in a medium-size saucepan. Add the shallot and sauté until translucent, just 2 or 3 minutes. Add the cauliflower and chicken stock (and the kosher salt, if using premade broth) and bring to a boil. Cook the cauliflower for 10 minutes, until very soft. Turn the heat down to low and, using the back of a wooden spoon, break up some of the florets. You're certainly not trying to puree anything here, but just to make it feel more souplike.
3. Stir in the butter. When it's melted, add the cumin seeds and parsley, and taste for salt and pepper. Serve right away.

TIME: *15 minutes*
FEEDS: *2 tired travelers*

NOT ON LOVE ALONE

Chicken Soup
with Ginger, Barley, and Chestnuts

This is the most complicated of the soups, only because it has the most ingredients. But it's really quite easy to make, and the broth, perfumed with ginger and star anise, is addictive.

4 cups homemade chicken stock (boxed low-sodium stock can be substituted)

½ lb. skinned and boned chicken thighs (about 2 thighs)

2 tablespoons pearl barley

1½ teaspoons kosher salt (if using home-made stock, which is unsalted; if using premade broth, taste for salt first)

½ cup chestnuts, either canned or jarred (my preference)

1 teaspoon peeled, julienned fresh ginger

½ star anise

1 scallion, sliced thinly on the bias, white and light green parts only

Sea salt and pepper, to taste

A bit of Bartlett or Anjou pear, cut into matchsticks (optional, for garnish)

1. Place the stock, chicken, and barley in a medium saucepan over high heat. If using homemade stock, add the salt. As soon as it's at a gentle boil, cover the pot and reduce the heat to low. Let the chicken and barley cook, covered, for 30 minutes.
2. Uncover the pot and take a look inside. The barley should have blossomed and be almost tender. Fish the chicken thighs out and, using a fork or the tip of a paring knife, pull the thighs apart into medium-size chunks. The meat should come apart pretty easily. Return the meat to the soup pot.
3. Break the chestnuts into pieces with your fingers, and add them to the pot along with the ginger, star anise, and scallion. Cook, uncovered, at a simmer for another 10 minutes.
4. Test for salt and pepper, then ladle into bowls. Add a few matchsticks of pear, if you're using it (I highly recommend it—the sweetness and tenderness bring out the ginger in the soup). Eat up as fast as you can spoon it into your mouth.

TIME: *45 minutes*
FEEDS: 2

Winter Pantry

THERE ARE QUITE a few more must-haves in my winter pantry than in my summer pantry. I think this is because (a) it's cold outside and I don't want to have to run out to the store all the time, and (b) we eat more in the winter. Seriously, I think it's because, considering the ripeness of vegetables in the height of summer, you don't need to fuss with them so much. A bit of herb, a squeeze of lemon, and you're good to go. In the winter, a greater depth of flavor is called for. Here is a list of both straight pantry items and some vegetables that are always in my fridge:

Lentils: Both regular brown lentils and the tiny, moss-green Le Puy lentils make the cut.

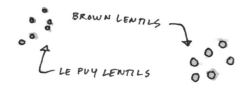

Dried Beans: Such as cannellini, kidney, garbanzo, and cranberry. For salads and hearty soups and stews.

Dried Mushrooms: Especially dried morels, which add such flavor to risotto and stews. Simply soak them in hot water and make sure they're free of sand.

Shredded Cabbage: I like red and Savoy cabbage, and it's easier to store shredded in resealable bags, ready to be sautéed or braised.

Brussels Sprouts: Maybe my favorite vegetable. Best way to prepare them? Sliced in half, sautéed with garlic and olive oil.

NOT ON LOVE ALONE

Hearty Greens: Such as kale or beet greens. I like to sauté them, much as I would Brussels sprouts, but you can also bake the stalks with Parmesan cheese.

Chestnuts: I prefer chestnuts that are vacuum-packed in jars, rather than the sort canned in water; they're firmer and more flavorful. You can use them in soups or roast them alongside pork spare ribs.

Interesting Root Vegetables: An occasional celery root, salsify, or parsnip will make its way home with me from the green market. They're great roasted next to meats.

DECEMBER

The Big Payback

The Big Payback

Remember, once upon a time, you had friends. These were people you went to the movies with, ate at diners with, drank at dive bars with, and who, most recently, paid many bucks to schlep to your wedding, stay in the local Discomfort Inn, and complete your set of sterling-silver dinner forks.

Of course, you haven't seen them recently. You've been busy at home, buying a new hamper together, dealing with your new joint bank accounts, et cetera. But now, it's payback time. You have the new home. It's filled to choking with shiny new tchotchkes, and it's time to put them to good use. That's right. It's time to have a party.

The best sort of cocktail party to have at home is the party where your guests can graze, moving from cozy spot to cozy spot in your living room while sampling all the good eats. You can bring things out in waves: the nuts, chickpeas, and cheese puffs first, followed by the hot (or warm) hors d'oeuvres when the party gets rocking. Finally, when you want to signal that things should wind up soon, bring out dessert. Then bring out the wheelbarrow to cart your guests out the door.

Payback Party Eats

SPICED PECANS (PAGE 206)

SPICY CHICKPEAS (PAGE 207)

MINI MOROCCAN PASTILLAS (PAGE 208)

GOUGÈRES (CHEESE PUFFS) (PAGE 210)

FRIED VEGGIES (PAGE 214)

WATER CHESTNUTS WRAPPED IN BACON (PAGE 218)

CRÈME BRÛLÉE ECLAIRS (PAGE 220)

Winter Tipples

FORTIFIED PIMM'S (PAGE 224)

THE STINKING BISHOP (PAGE 225)

THE WEEKENDER (PAGE 227)

REAL TOM COLLINS (PAGE 227)

Spiced Pecans

I like these with a little kick of heat—the half teaspoon of cayenne pepper is the high end of polite spiciness. If you want a tamer nut, use one-quarter teaspoon.

4 cups pecan halves

1 egg white

1 teaspoon kosher salt

1 tablespoon crushed, dried rosemary leaves

½ teaspoon cayenne pepper (or to taste)

½ teaspoon ground cumin

2 tablespoons light brown sugar

Nonstick cooking spray, to grease the sheet pan

1. Preheat the oven to 325°F.
2. Spread out the nuts in an even layer on a rimmed baking sheet, and pop them into the oven for 5 to 7 minutes, until lightly toasted.
3. Meanwhile, put the egg white in a medium-size mixing bowl and whisk lightly to break up the albumen. Add the salt, the spices and the sugar, and whisk to combine. When you remove the nuts from the oven, let them cool for a moment, then add them to the spice mixture and coat them evenly. Spray the cookie sheet with the nonstick cooking spray, put them back on the cookie sheet in an even layer and bake for another 20 to 22 minutes, until lacquered with the spices and a lovely mahogany brown. Let them cool before you serve them or transfer them to an airtight container.

TIME: *35 minutes*
FEEDS: *This recipe makes 4 cups of nuts, enough for 16 noshers.*

Spicy Chickpeas

Here's another kick of heat: the more heat your snacks give off, the more people drink and the more festive your party becomes. Capisce? You can actually get a version of these at Indian grocery stores (that's how I first tried them), but making them at home is easy enough.

1 cup dried chickpeas	¼ teaspoon cayenne pepper
½ teaspoon curry powder	Pinch of kosher salt
¼ teaspoon paprika	Neutral vegetable oil (safflower or canola) for deep frying

1. Either soak the chickpeas in cold water overnight, or pour boiling water over them and soak for 1½ hours, depending on how much you've planned ahead. When they're softened, pat them dry thoroughly.
2. Fill a deep saucepan with vegetable oil about a third of the way up. Set up the frying thermometer so the probe is in the oil but not touching the sides or bottom of the pan. Heat the oil to 350°F. While it's heating, fill a rimmed baking sheet with a layer of crumpled paper towels.
3. Fry the chickpeas in batches, 3 minutes per batch. Scoop them out with a bamboo-handled strainer or a slotted spoon and let them drain on the paper towels. When you've done all the chickpeas, refry them in batches for another 3 minutes per batch, until slightly golden.
4. Drain the chickpeas again, then transfer them to a bowl. In another small bowl, combine the curry, paprika, cayenne pepper, and salt, then sprinkle this mixture over the chickpeas. Let cool, then serve.

SPECIAL EQUIPMENT: *A candy or frying thermometer, to monitor the hot oil*
TIME: *Some unattended time soaking the chickpeas, but only a few minutes of working time*
FEEDS: *Makes about 2 cups of chickpeas, enough for two dishes scattered about the party*

Mini Moroccan Pastillas

The most complicated recipe in this chapter, but it's stunning and easily made ahead. Everybody will think they're those tired old spinach-stuffed phyllo triangles and get a delicious surprise instead. JS has been known to eat half a batch in one sitting, before the guests arrive, pleasing himself if not his wife.

1 lb. skinless, boneless chicken thighs

1 clove garlic, minced

¼ cup finely chopped fresh flat-leaf parsley

1 shallot, minced

A pinch of saffron

¼ teaspoon ground ginger

½ teaspoon ground cinnamon

1 stick unsalted butter

½ cup water

Pinch of kosher salt and pepper

2 eggs, lightly beaten

A squeeze of lemon juice—about lemon's worth

½ cup whole, blanched almonds

2 tablespoons confectioners' sugar, plus extra for serving

1 lb. package phyllo dough leaves (available in the frozen-food section of the supermarket)

1. Put the chicken thighs, garlic, 2 tablespoons of parsley, shallot, saffron, ground ginger, ¼ teaspoon of the ground cinnamon, and 1 tablespoon of the butter in a medium-size saucepan along with ½ cup water, a pinch of salt, and a grinding of pepper. Bring the pot to a boil over medium heat, cover, and turn down the heat to low. Simmer the contents for 45 minutes, or until the chicken thighs are extremely tender and falling apart.

2. Remove the chicken from the pot, and set aside to cool. Meanwhile, turn up the heat and reduce the sauce by half, about 4 to 5 minutes. When you've done that, turn the heat back down to medium-low, and add the eggs, along with the squeeze of lemon juice, stirring the whole time. Cook the egg mixture until any excess moisture has boiled away—it should look like scrambled eggs when you're done, about 5 to 7 minutes more. Turn off the heat and transfer the eggs to a mixing bowl.

3. Shred the chicken thighs and add the meat to the mixing bowl, along with the remaining 2 tablespoons of parsley. Taste for salt. Mix to combine, then put in the fridge to cool.

NOT ON LOVE ALONE

4. In a small, dry frying pan over moderate heat, or in your toaster oven, toast the almonds until golden. Place them in the bowl of a food processor or blender along with the powdered sugar and remaining ¼ teaspoon cinnamon. Blend until it looks like fine crumbs. (Alternatively, you can chop the almonds fine with a chef's knife, then mix almonds, sugar, and cinnamon together in a bowl.)
5. Preheat the oven to 350°F.
6. Melt the remaining butter in the microwave and have it close at hand. Have the chicken mixture, a teaspoon, and the almond mixture standing by. Grease two baking sheets.
7. Prepare the phyllo. Phyllo is, to put it nicely, problematic. It'll make sailors of us all, language-wise. My best advice is, once you've taken it from the package and unrolled it, cover it immediately with a slightly damp kitchen towel and never let it see fresh air. Take out 2 sheets of phyllo from under its damp tent, and separate them. Brush one layer with butter, then place another sheet on top of that, and brush it with butter. Start at the corners and work your way to the middle—the phyllo stays put better that way. Cut the layered phyllo lengthwise into 3-inch-long strips.
8. Starting at one end of a strip of phyllo, place 1 teaspoon of chicken on the phyllo and top it with a hearty pinch (about ½ teaspoon) of the almonds. Place the filling at an angle so that you can fold the pastry over it and create the beginnings of a triangle. Keep folding the phyllo over itself, creating one triangle after another, like folding a flag. When you've folded the whole thing up, brush it with another bit of butter, then place it on the baking sheet.
9. Repeat steps 7 and 8 until all the phyllo and filling are used up.
10. Pop the *pastillas* in the oven and bake for 15 minutes, or until golden. These can be made ahead of time, and reheated in a low oven at party time.
11. To serve, sift a touch of confectioners' sugar over the top and cut the *pastillas* in half for easier eating.

SPECIAL EQUIPMENT: *A food processor is nice, but not necessary.*
A pastry brush, however, is necessary.
TIME: *2 hours, some of it unattended*
FEEDS: *Makes 36 pastillas*

Gougères (Cheese Puffs)

always make these. They are a snap—as long as you have all the ingredients on the counter, ready to go when you start—and though the recipe makes many, they're easily frozen and reheated in my favorite appliance, the toaster oven.

1 cup water or chicken stock (homemade or canned)

1 stick unsalted butter, cut into a few pieces

1 teaspoon kosher salt

1 cup flour

4 eggs, plus 1 for an egg wash

1½ cups grated Gruyère or Swiss cheese

Sea salt

1. Preheat the oven to 375°F. Line 2 rimmed baking sheets with parchment paper.
2. Put the stock, butter, and salt in a medium-size saucepan, and bring to a boil over high heat, stirring with a wooden spoon. As soon as all the butter is melted and the stock is rolling, turn off the heat and dump all the flour in the pot. Give the mixture a good wallop with a wooden spoon until all the lumps are gone and the mixture is smooth, like paste. Put the pot back over a low flame, stirring constantly, for about a minute (you want to dry out the dough slightly).
3. Transfer the hot dough to the bowl of a standing mixer or another mixing bowl. On medium speed, incorporate the 4 eggs, one after the other, beating in between each addition until the eggs are completely incorporated. The dough should be a smooth, sunny yellow, and still quite warm. Add the shredded cheese and mix to combine.
4. Fill a pastry bag or zip-top bag (see Pastry Bag Ins and Outs, page 212) with the *gougère* dough, and pipe out tablespoon-size amounts, about 1 inch apart, in long rows on the baking sheet.
5. When all the dough is piped out, mix the remaining egg with 1 teaspoon of water to make an egg wash. Then, using a small pastry brush or (my preference) a clean finger, daub the tops of the little mounds of dough with some egg wash. Follow that with a nice sprinkling of sea salt.
6. Bake the puffs for 10 minutes at 375° F, then lower the heat to 325°F and bake for 15 to 20 minutes more, or until the puffs are golden brown. Try to resist taking a peek for at least the first 15 minutes, or the *gougères* may not reach the majestic heights desired. Serve warm. (These are easily made ahead and frozen— just reheat them in a low oven for 5 minutes.)

NOT ON LOVE ALONE

SPECIAL EQUIPMENT: *If you're feeling very fancy, you need a standing mixer and a pastry bag fitted with a ½-inch tip. But the truth is, you can make these with a hand mixer, or even a wooden spoon, and a zip-top bag for the piping.*

TIME: *40 minutes*

FEEDS: *This recipe makes about 50 cheese puffs.*

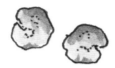

⌣ A NOTE ON BUTTER ⌣

J USE ONLY UNSALTED butter, because it's what I grew up with. It's handy to cook with—and an absolute to bake with—because you can control how much salt there is going into your recipe.

For buttering bread, I like French butter, which has a higher milk-fat content than regular butter—and more milk fat means more flavor. That's just the way it is.

SALTED

SWEET
(THIS IS WHAT
I USE)

FANCY FRENCH BUTTER
- for -
SPECIAL OCCASIONS

Pastry Bag Ins and Outs

$\mathcal{I}$T CAN TAKE a bit of time to get used to using a pastry bag. Here are some troubleshooting tips:

- You can make filling a pastry bag easier by resting it, tip down, in a drinking glass. That way both hands can concentrate on keeping the bag open and scooping in whatever you're piping.

- When the bag is full, give it a good jog or two to remove any air bubbles from within. This will prevent any embarrassing piping-bag explosions.

- Pipe with two hands. Twist the top of the bag closed with your dominant hand, and use it to keep constant pressure on the filling so it comes out at an even rate. The other hand can guide the tip.

- Practice a few times and expect a few mistakes.

Making a zip-top pastry bag: Just fill the bag with whatever you need to pipe, and seal it, forcing any excess air out of the bag. Cut off one corner to the aperture you need and pipe away. Best part? Easy cleanup.

FOR EASE
-of-
FILLING

WATER
GLASS

USE BOTH HANDS

TEST SQUIRT

ZIP-TOP
BAG

CUT HERE

Fried Veggies

Who doesn't like fried things? Certainly I like them, as this book has illustrated. These veggies can be made earlier in the day, kept at room temperature, and served au naturel or with a little dip, such as a light tomato sauce, a yogurt-dill sauce, or just a bit of crème fraîche with lemon juice and parsley.

I'm including two batters here, one with cheese and one without. I've suggested some vegetables that hold up well in batter, but feel free to experiment: look at the art on page 215 for suggestions.

FOR THE VEGETABLES:

2 bulbs fennel, washed and trimmed, cut into ¼-inch slices

½ head cauliflower, washed and trimmed into medium-size florets

1 sweet potato or butternut squash, peeled and shredded on a box grater

FOR THE SIMPLE BATTER:

⅓ cup all-purpose flour

¼ cup seltzer water

Pinch of kosher salt

FOR THE FANCY BATTER:

⅓ cup all-purpose flour

¼ cup seltzer water

Pinch of kosher salt

1 egg

⅓ cup finely grated Parmesan cheese

1 tablespoon finely chopped fresh flat-leaf parsley

Neutral oil (such as canola or safflower), for frying

Sea salt and lemon wedges, for serving

1. Get a steamer going on the stove. First steam the fennel for 3 minutes, then the cauliflower for 4 minutes. Let the vegetables cool on paper towels.
2. Prepare the simple batter: Sift the flour into a medium-size bowl, then slowly whisk in the seltzer. Add the salt. Then, in a separate bowl, prepare the fancy batter: Repeat the previous steps with the flour, seltzer, and salt, then add the egg and mix gently until completely combined. Fold in the cheese and parsley.
3. Heat a large skillet over a medium flame. Fill the skillet ¼ inch deep with vegetable oil and heat until shimmering. Test the heat by dropping a bit of bread into the oil. If it sizzles and browns within 20 seconds, it's ready to go. Prepare a cookie rack by placing it over paper towels.
4. Start with the fennel. Dip it in the simple batter, letting any excess drip back into the bowl, and lay it gently into the hot oil, leading away from your body to pre-

NOT ON LOVE ALONE

vent splatters. Continue adding the fennel without crowding the pan (you may need to cook it in batches), turning it once, until it's golden brown. Retrieve the fennel with tongs or a strainer, and then let cool on the cookie rack.

5. Next, the cauliflower. Using the fancy batter, dip and fry the cauliflower pieces as you did the fennel, regulating the heat under the skillet if things are getting too brown too quickly. Drain them the same way.

6. Finally, the sweet potato. Mix the shredded sweet potato with the remaining fancy batter. Transfer heaping tablespoonfuls to the hot oil, frying them until they're golden brown on each side. These will take a bit longer than the other vegetables, about 7 minutes a side, because you want to be sure that the potato cooks completely. Make sure the little patties aren't too thick—press them down if they're taller than they are wide. These should be drained on the cookie rack, too.

7. The nicest way to serve these is in mounds on parchment paper, with sea salt and lemon wedges on the side. If you can serve them hot, that's great, but I find them just as delicious warm or at room temperature.

SPECIAL EQUIPMENT: *A bamboo-handled strainer or tongs for flipping and removing the fried vegetables*
TIME: *A good bit of time for the prepping and frying in batches—at least 40 minutes*
FEEDS: *This recipe makes about 50 pieces.*

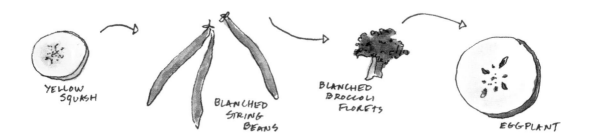

YELLOW SQUASH

BLANCHED STRING BEANS

BLANCHED BROCCOLI FLORETS

EGGPLANT

Winter Entertaining

∞

IN THE WINTER, particularly around the holidays, the food needs to be copious, the drinks generous, and the lighting flattering. While in the summer we all look good with our late-summer tans in the fading sunlight, by December, the best of us need some nicely dimmed lights and the flicker of dozens of votive candles. And, instead of festooning the entire place in Douglas fir, why not buy lots of tulips, which are everywhere in December, in one color, strip off their leaves, and lean them in great bunches in glass vases?

It's nicer to start cocktails a bit earlier than in the summer, since the sun disappears so early and, baby, it gets cold outside late.

In terms of food, I like a good variety (as is evident here) scattered about a room so people don't all congregate in one place. These recipes, plus a few cheeses, some long breadsticks, and maybe some charcuterie—cured ham and the like—would make for plenty of food for your guests on a long night of snacking and talking.

As for alcohol, I suggest (as I did in the summer) limiting the selection to one drink with the hard stuff, plus a selection of wine and beer. December nights lend themselves particularly well to bubbly things.

At a party with a larger spread, a bit of dessert is a welcome addition. The éclairs here are a real showstopper, but anything—cupcakes, brownies—will be hoovered up by the assembled hordes.

If you're thinking of having a New Year's party, even if it's at home, I would send out invitations (real letters! real stamps!) and suggest a dress code. We wear jeans the rest of the year—on one night we can look respectable.

Water Chestnuts Wrapped in Bacon

These couldn't be more old-fashioned. A fancier version of this recipe calls for wrapping the bacon around sea scallops, but I believe that's a waste of perfectly good sea scallops. The water chestnuts are easier and significantly cheaper, and the sweet crunch is lovely with the smoky bacon. It would be a good idea to assign the task of making these to whoever is less handy in the kitchen, since it's just manual labor.

1 (8-ounce) package thin-cut bacon   1 (8-ounce) can whole water chestnuts

1. Preheat the oven to 400°F.
2. Cut several strips of bacon into 3-inch lengths. Drain the water chestnuts and wrap each one in a length of bacon, securing the bacon with a toothpick. Put the water chestnuts on a rimmed baking sheet.
3. Slide the sheet into the oven and bake for 15 minutes, or until the bacon has rendered and is crispy. Pull from the oven, drain on paper towels, and serve hot.

SPECIAL EQUIPMENT: *Toothpicks!*
TIME: *20 minutes*
FEEDS: *This makes about 25 bacon-wrapped chestnuts.*

Fromage!

a Cheese Play in Five Acts

ACT FIVE: Party of Five

SCENE: *Saturday afternoon. J rushes into Murray's Cheese shop and makes a beeline for the counter. After she waits impatiently on line, CIELO finally has time for her.*

J, *desperately*. I need party cheese!

CIELO, *calm, collected*. For how many people, lady? Three hundred?

J. Almost! Twenty-five!

CIELO. What about a platter of five cheeses?

J, *nervous*. But which ones? Can you just pick them out?

CIELO. Of course. I'll give you a blue, Great Hill, from Massachusetts. And a nice creamy French Pierre Robert. And this Dutch Roomano, it's hard like Parmesan. A nice American goat, Humboldt Fog. And a sheep's-milk from the Pyrenees, Petit Basque. OK, lady? I'll just put you down for five hundred dollars' worth of cheese [wink].

J, *greatly relieved*. You're a lifesaver!

(*fin*)

For more on Murray's Cheese Shop, visit www.murrayscheese.com.

Crème Brûlée Éclairs

These éclairs are a great mix: there's the tenderness of the éclair shell, the sweet creaminess of the pastry cream, and the hard candy top. The flavors are the same as in crème brûlée, but no blowtorch is necessary. Though it does take some time to make them, once you get the hang of the piping there's nothing too difficult about the process. The best piece of advice I can give is that you have all your ingredients measured and at hand before you start—things go quickly and you don't want to find yourself having to run to the fridge in the middle of the recipe.

FOR THE PASTRY CREAM:

2 cups whole milk

½ vanilla bean, split lengthwise

6 egg yolks

⅔ cup sugar

¼ cup cornstarch

1 teaspoon cold unsalted butter

FOR THE ÉCLAIR SHELLS:

½ cup water

½ cup whole milk

1½ teaspoons sugar

½ teaspoon salt

1 stick butter, cubed

1 cup all-purpose flour

4 eggs

FOR THE TOP:

1¼ cup sugar

⅓ cup water

Prepare the pastry cream:

1. In a medium-size saucepan, heat the milk with the split vanilla bean until it comes to a boil. Keep an eye on it—this is not the time to learn how quickly milk can boil over and make a mess on your stove. As soon as it boils, cover the pan and turn off the heat, setting the milk aside for 10 minutes to steep.

2. In a large bowl, beat together the egg yolks and sugar with a mixer until they're lemon-colored and increased in bulk, about 3 minutes. Whisk in the cornstarch until no lumps remain.

3. Quickly incorporate ½ cup of the milk into the egg base (this, for the technical-minded among us, is called tempering and it prevents the shock of the hot milk from curdling the eggs, a bummer indeed). Once that ½ cup is incorporated, mix in the remaining milk in a steady stream, then pour everything *back* into the pot, through a sieve to catch the vanilla beans and any lumps of cornstarch. Stir

the whole shebang continually over medium heat until the mixture begins to thicken and comes to a lazy boil, probably no more than 2 minutes. Be diligent in your stirring. When it has thickened, turn off the heat and swirl in the pat of butter. Transfer the pastry cream to a bowl and cover with plastic wrap, pressing the wrap directly onto the surface of the cream to prevent a film from forming. When it's cool, place it in the fridge for several hours or overnight.

Make the éclair shells:

1. Preheat the oven to 375°F. Line two rimmed cookie sheets with parchment paper.
2. It is absolutely imperative to have everything ready here, because this dough goes fast. In a medium-size saucepan, heat the water, milk, sugar, salt, and butter over high heat, stirring with a wooden spoon until the liquid is boiling and the butter has melted. Turn off the heat and immediately dump in the entire cup of flour, mixing energetically with the wooden spoon until the contents of the pot look like a smooth paste. Turn the heat back on to low and stir the dough continuously for 1 minute, letting the mixture dry out a bit. Then, transfer it to the bowl of a standing mixer or another mixing bowl placed close to your hand mixer. One by one, incorporate the eggs, making sure to beat the dough thoroughly before adding the next. The final result should be a smooth, shiny, slightly marigold-colored dough.
3. Fill your piping bag, fitted with a ½-inch tip, with the batter, and start piping little logs—about 1 inch wide and 2½ inches long, placed about 2 inches apart from each other—onto the parchment-lined cookie sheets. This batch should make about thirty éclair shells.
4. When you're done piping, pop the éclair shells into the oven, resisting your urge to check them, for 10 minutes; then turn down the oven to 325°F and bake for another 15 to 20 minutes, until they're golden and puffy. Pull them out of the oven and let them cool on their trays.

Top and fill the éclairs:

1. Once everything is cool, fill your pastry bag with the pastry cream and set it aside in the refrigerator. Grease a cookie sheet and set it on the counter. Prepare a large ice bath by filling a mixing bowl or pan with ice cubes. Set it nearby on the counter as well.
2. Now, prepare the topping for the éclairs. Put the sugar in a small, heavy-bottomed saucepan (the sides should not be very high) and gently pour the water over it, running a finger through the sugar to make sure everything is moistened. Then don't touch it! Turn on the heat to medium-high and let the sugar water cook, gently swirling it once or twice until you have a nice amber caramel, about 10

minutes. Immediately take it off the heat and put the bottom of the pan in the ice bath for 30 seconds to stop the cooking. Take the pan out of the ice bath, move the ice bath away from your cooking surface, and start carefully dipping the éclair shells, tops down, into the (very, very hot) sugar and placing them, caramel side down, on the cookie sheet. I suggest using tongs to hold the éclair shells if you're nervous about getting your fingers close to hot sugar. If the caramel starts to harden, you can apply some more heat to the pot to loosen it up. The éclair tops will harden within minutes.

3. Finally, take the piping bag full of pastry cream, pick up a topped éclair, and, poking the tip in one end of the éclair, pipe a squirt of cream in the middle, without piping so much that it weighs a pound and explodes. Put the finished éclairs on a platter top side up and, once you've finished them all, cover and put them in the fridge until you're ready to eat.

SPECIAL EQUIPMENT: *A pastry bag with a metal tip (or a snipped zip-top bag—see Pastry Bag Ins and Outs, page 212); a hand-held or standing mixer; parchment paper for lining cookie sheets; an ice bath in a bowl large enough to hold the pot of hot sugar*
TIME: *About 1½ hours, including baking time*
FEEDS: *A recipe makes about 30 miniature éclairs.*

Éclair Variations

YOU DON'T NEED me to tell you that the world of éclairs is a large and varied one. Why don't you:

- Use the chocolate ganache recipe from February (page 40) to top the éclairs, instead of the caramel.
- Add 2 ounces of chopped, semisweet chocolate to the hot pastry cream to have . . . chocolate pastry cream. Or add a little instant espresso to that for mocha pastry cream.
- You can fill the éclairs with orange or lemon curd, too.
- Why not make a quick icing (water, confectioners' sugar, almond extract) and dip the tops in that, then in toasted, slivered almonds.
- Or, in the springtime, crush some strawberries in confectioners' sugar with a drop of water, and have strawberry éclairs.

You can tell I'm a serious éclair scholar.

WINTER TIPPLES

I think I've mentioned before that I don't drink hard alcohol very often, and when I forget myself and do, I am always very, very sorry. But that doesn't mean our friends shouldn't wake up the day after a party with pounding headaches and blurry vision!

Also included here is a list of single-malt Scotches recommended by my friend Weatherly Ralph, whom I've quoted in part, à la *Zagat*, on page 226.

~

Fortified Pimm's

Pimm's is a terrific summertime drink, a sort of British sangria, but I think this version, with the extra kick of vodka and the concentration on oranges and lemons, makes it a great wintertime drink, too.

2 cups Pimm's

2 cups San Pellegrino Limonata (a tart, fizzy drink)

½ cup any decent vodka

1 orange, sectioned (see page 101)

1 grapefruit, sectioned (see page 101)

1 lemon, thinly sliced

½ Granny Smith apple, cored and cut into thin crescents

Gently stir together all of the ingredients in a large pitcher, and serve in tumblers over lots of ice.

~

QUENCHES: *The thirst of 6*

NOT ON LOVE ALONE

The Stinking Bishop

A hot drink with a spectacular presentation. I don't know where the name comes from, as the stinking bishop is also a (indeed very stinky) cheese. I assume this drink has English origins, and suggests that your average British bishop is not only lacking in personal hygiene, but drunk as a lord as well.

2 lemons	½ cup Cognac
1 cup superfine sugar	2¼ cups boiling water
1 cup dark rum	

1. Zest and juice the lemons and set the juice aside. In a large flameproof bowl (or punch bowl) mix together the zest, sugar, and dark rum.
2. Put the Cognac in a flameproof measuring cup or pan. Heat the Cognac for 30 seconds in the microwave, or on top of the stove for a minute. If you've heated it on a stove, remove it from the heat and any flame. Then, carefully, flambé it with a match and pour it into the bowl. Add the boiling water and reserved lemon juice, and serve hot in little punch cups.

QUENCHES: *12 revelers*

Weatherly's Single-Malt List

J COULDN'T TELL a single-malt Scotch from bathtub gin, so I turned to my friend Weatherly Ralph for advice. She has spent enough time in the UK, throwing down shots with lords and locals alike, to know what she is talking about.

In fact, the only time I've gotten close to single-malt Scotch was with Weath, while she was a graduate student at Oxford. I happened to eat dinner with her in the hall at Christ Church College on Robbie Burns night, which involves some poetry reading, some haggis with neeps and tatties (recipes decidedly not included here), and lots of single-malt to wash it all down with. The last thing I remember is dancing to Duran Duran's "The Reflex"—a lower form of poetic expression than Burns's "To a Mouse," perhaps, but just as compelling in its way.

Here are a few Weatherly reviews of single-malt Scotches:

Laphroaig 10-Year-Old Scotch: "Very salty and peaty," this lively Scotch from the island of Islay in Scotland is a bona fide "man drink," meant to be sipped slowly on the coldest nights of the year. Best neat or with a little water.

Edradour Single Malt: From Great Britain's smallest distillery "in the Highlands" comes this "lighter" "delicious" Scotch, with berry notes and a rich, gold hue. Best of all? "Ladies can drink it."

Cragganmore Single Malt (12 Year): "A good all-around Scotch" for single-malt neophytes, this "fragrant" Scotch has some sweet notes to offset the anticipated burn.

Macallan (12 Year): Aged in sherry oak, it's a robust, spicy Scotch. It's no wonder that "older men love this one."

The Weekender

*This was a drink invented by our friend Joe Piech on vacation . . .
when you have all day to invent things like this. And drink things like this.*

2 cups freshly squeezed orange juice

1 cup club soda

1 cup gin, of a decent variety

Orange slices, to float on the top

In a large pitcher, gently stir together the orange juice, club soda, and gin. Pour over ice and add a slim slice of orange to each drink.

QUENCHES: *6 drinkers*

Real Tom Collins

This version comes from a friend who has a masters in mixology from a course he took at Yale University. Well, I don't know if it was an accredited course, but I like to think so.

¼ cup good gin

2 tablespoons freshly squeezed lemon juice

1 teaspoon superfine sugar

⅓ cup club soda

Add the gin, lemon juice, and sugar to a cocktail shaker with some ice and shake, baby. Strain it into a cocktail glass filled with ice and add the club soda.

QUENCHES: *Just 1. Multiply ad infinitum.*

ANNIVERSARY

And Many More

And Many More

STILL CLAIMS that the first multicourse, complicated meal I cooked him—for an early "anniversary" of ours—is the best thing I've ever made. Though sometimes exasperated by this sentiment—I think of the hundreds of my meals he's eaten between then and now—I'm always touched by his dogged insistence. It's the romance of the thing.

That meal was entirely made out of Julia Child's *Mastering the Art of French Cooking,* and included such fussy standbys as lobster with mayonnaise and beef tenderloin with cèpes. In honor of it, I've made the main course here lobster, though with slightly less mayo and grated tomalley involved.

The meal should be easy, and not dreadfully heavy, though it depends on how overboard you go on the foie gras. After all, the point of an anniversary dinner is to admire each other and impress yourselves with how lucky you are.

And though I seem to pop the cork in a bottle of Champagne at the least provocation, if there's any time to drink some, it's now.

Here's to a year . . .
and many more

FOIE GRAS WITH BRIOCHE (PAGE 232)

&

LOBSTER GRATINÉED WITH HERB BUTTER (PAGE 234)

&

BRAISED BOSTON LETTUCE HEARTS (PAGE 236)

&

CHOCOLATE POTS DE CRÈME (PAGE 237)

Foie Gras with Brioche

There's absolutely no cooking involved here, only assembling.

Foie gras: Of goose, please, not duck. Either a mousse of foie gras, which is a less-expensive pâté, or (what's much better) the pricier terrine of foie gras, where the whole lobes are cooked together. This is beyond delicious, and it's so rich you can get a very small amount. The best source for this is D'Artagnan, a company based in New Jersey, and the smallest portion they sell of the terrine is half a pound, which is, in the words of my mother, a plentiful sufficiency for two people (www.dartagnan.com).

Brioche: The best bakery around will have little individual brioches, or a small loaf, which you should slice into sandwich-bread thickness and toast well. In a pinch, you could use a good-quality challah (though the idea makes me weep).

Unsalted butter: Because there's not enough fat in the foie gras as it is. Buy the fanciest French butter from Normandy you can find.

Sea salt: Need I say this should be the sort of salt that has a better pedigree than most of the dogs at the Westminster Dog Show?

Presentation: Just slice a good slab of chilled terrine of foie gras and lay it on a plate, served with a few curls of butter and a small pile of sea salt. Serve the toasted brioche on a small plate on the side.

TIME: *Mere moments*
FEEDS: *2 lucky souls*

Foie Gras Go-Withs

∞

TRADITIONALLY, FOIE GRAS is paired with Sauternes, a concentrated sweet wine, or other sweet wines. You can get versions of these sweet white wines across the price spectrum and from California, France, and Italy. The best part is that they're widely available in half bottles, perfect for two.

Pops, who knows his wine, recommends the modestly priced Vin de Glacière by California producer Bonny Doon.

Sides for Foie Gras

If you want to gild the lily, you could serve dainty portions of the following:

- Fig preserves
- Red currant jelly
- Toasted, chopped hazelnuts
- Thin slices of Anjou pear
- A few sliced prunes
- Shaved black truffle
- A small pool of very high-quality balsamic vinegar

Lobster Gratinéed with Herb Butter

*H*ow much work you do on this dish is a question of how much control you want over the lobster. At fancier markets and fish stores, you can get lobsters presteamed, which keeps you from having to send the big fellas to their death yourself. It does, however, keep you from being in control of how cooked (or, sadly, overcooked) the lobster is. The final decision is up to you.

FOR THE LOBSTERS:

2 live lobsters—make sure they're very lively—each about 1½ pounds

Kosher salt

FOR THE COMPOUND BUTTER:

4 tablespoons unsalted butter, very soft

1 tablespoon finely chopped fresh flat-leaf parsley

1 teaspoon finely snipped fresh chives

½ teaspoon finely chopped fresh tarragon

1 teaspoon lemon zest

½ teaspoon kosher salt

Chopped fresh flat-leaf parsley, for garnish

1. If you're taking care of the lobster business yourself, put the critters in a bowl and place them in your freezer for at least 30 minutes to induce a lobstery coma.
2. Meanwhile, bring a large pot of salted water to a boil over high heat. Make sure the pot has a lid that fits. When the water is really rolling, slide the chilly lobsters into the water, where they will immediately start turning red. When the water comes back to a boil, cook the lobsters for 12 minutes. Pull them from the water and let cool. You can do this earlier in the day and refrigerate the cooked lobsters until you need them.
3. While the lobsters are cooling off, make the compound butter. Mix all the ingredients in a small bowl with a rubber spatula, then scrape the whole mess onto a piece of waxed paper. Roll up the butter in the paper and shape into a log. Pop it into the freezer to let it set up, for at least 15 minutes (you can make it ahead and keep it there, but move it to the fridge to soften before using it).
4. Preheat the broiler.
5. Cut the lobsters in half along the axis of their bodies, so each half has a claw and the cross-section of a tail. Pull out the not-so-nice contents of the head and chest cavity, and scrape out the green tomalley. Crack the claws and pull out the meat, placing it in the now cleaned chest cavity, along with any meat you get out of the joints. Arrange it so it looks pretty, but make sure it's not sticking up too

far, or you might have an unhappy result in the broiler. You can prepare this several hours in advance and keep, covered, in the fridge. Take them out of the cold for half an hour to take the chill off before you pop them into the broiler.

6. Place each half (4 total) cut side up on a broiling pan or rimmed baking sheet. Top each half with a quarter of the herb butter, making sure to get a bit on the claw meat. Slide the pan into the broiler and broil until the butter is melted and there's some nice golden color on the tail, about 3 to 5 minutes.

7. Pull the lobsters from the broiler and arrange them prettily on a plate, dusting them with parsley. Serve them with Braised Boston Lettuce Hearts (recipe follows).

TIME: *Just a few minutes to prepare the butter and broil the lobster, another 20 minutes if you plan on cooking the lobster yourself*
FEEDS: *2 in a celebratory mood*

Braised Boston Lettuce Hearts

Sometimes you can find very small heads of Boston lettuce, which are perfect for this. If not, buy a larger head and take off some of the outer leaves so you get to the pale green heart. Braising is an overstatement here; it's more of a somersault in lemon and cream in a pan before joining the lobster on the plate.

4 tiny, or 2 small heads Boston lettuce, washed and dried, a few outer leaves removed, but kept intact—trim and discard any browned parts at the base (the end result should be 2 hearts, each about the size of a softball)

1 teaspoon butter

3 tablespoons heavy cream

1 tablespoon fresh lemon juice

1 teaspoon lemon zest

Sea salt and freshly ground black pepper

Cut the lettuce hearts in half lengthwise. Heat a medium-size skillet over high heat. Melt the butter, let the foaming subside, and then add the cream, lemon juice, lemon zest, and some salt and grindings of pepper. Add the lettuce hearts and swirl them about the pan, flipping them over with tongs until the outer leaves just start to wilt, about 30 seconds. Serve with the lobster.

TIME: *Just a minute or two in a hot pan*
FEEDS: *2 lovebirds*

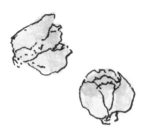

NOT ON LOVE ALONE

Chocolate Pots de Crème

hese rich custards will make you happy without weighing you down.

2 cups half-and-half	6 egg yolks
½ vanilla bean, split	⅓ cup sugar
2 ounces high-quality semisweet chocolate, such as Lindt, chopped	¼ cup sifted Dutch-process cocoa powder

1. Preheat the oven to 325°F.

2. Bring the half-and-half to a simmer in a small saucepan with the vanilla bean; cover the pan and turn off the heat. Wait for 5 minutes, then rescue the vanilla pod from the pot. Turn on the heat to low and add the chopped semisweet chocolate, whisking until the chocolate is completely melted. Turn off the heat, cover, and set aside for a moment.

3. In a medium-size mixing bowl, whisk the egg yolks with the sugar until lemon-colored and light; then whisk in the cocoa powder until just combined, without lumps. Whisking continually and furiously, add ½ cup of the hot chocolate half-and-half to the eggs to temper them. Then, add the remaining chocolate half-and-half to the egg mixture. Strain the custard through a sieve into another mixing bowl, making sure no bits of egg yolk get into the bowl.

4. Ladle the chocolate custard into the ramekins or pots, dividing it evenly among them. If using ramekins, cover the tops with a bit of tinfoil to prevent a skin from forming during baking. Put a roasting pan in the oven and place the ramekins in it. Carefully pour boiling water into the pan until there's ½ inch around the ramekins.

5. Bake these little custards for 25 minutes, or until they are mostly set but still a little wobbly in the middle. Overbaking makes them too dense—the chocolate flavor is intense, but the texture should be soft and light. They're perfect on their own, chilled from the refrigerator.

SPECIAL EQUIPMENT: *You need six 4-ounce ramekins or pots de crème*
TIME: *Less than an hour of work, plus time to let the pots cool in the fridge*
FEEDS: *This makes 6—a couple for the anniversary night and some for later.*

First-Anniversary Gifts

THE THEME IS paper, liberally interpreted:

- ✇ An early edition of a favorite book
- ✇ Personalized stationery
- ✇ Tickets to a play or a show
- ✇ A map of an upcoming vacation destination
- ✇ A print of a favorite painting or other work of art

Index

African Marinade, 102
alcohol, serving, 152, 217. *See also* beverages;
   cocktail parties
allspice, ideas for, 110
almonds, toasting, 144
Anniversary, 229–238
Apples, Sautéed, with Vanilla, 185
Applesauce, 26
Applesauce Cake, 76
Apricot-Thyme Clafouti, 130
April, 61–79
arborio rice, 8
Artichoke Hearts and Peas, Herb-Braised, 64
artichokes, 62, 66–67
Asian Marinade, 102
asparagus, 71
   roasted, 65
August, 133–154

Bacon, Water Chestnuts Wrapped in, 218
bain-marie water bath, 195
basil, 156, 163
   Farfalle with Ricotta, Lemon, Basil, and Peas,
     165
   Fusilli with Zucchini, Garlic, and Basil, 164
   Spaghetti Pesto with Croutons, 166
basmati rice, 8
beans, dried, 200. *See also* green beans
   as pie weights, 55
   in Soupe au Pistou, 116–118
   Spicy Chickpeas, 207
beef, 20, 121
   Rib of Beef on the Grill, 121
   Veal, Braised, with Mushroom Ragout and
     Garlic Toasts, 18
beets, steaming, 180
Belgian mussel pot, 58
Bellinis, 151
bento boxes, 188, 192
   Edamame, 192
   Fennel and Radish Salad, 193
   Frittata Wrap, 190
beverages
   Bellinis, 151
   Cava, 43
   Champagne, 42–43

orange juice and gin, 227
Pimm's, Fortified, 224
Pineapple Vodka Tonics, 154
Prosecco, 43
Single-Malt Scotch (list), 226
The Stinking Bishop, 225
Tom Collins, 227
wine, 60, 152
Blueberries, Relaxed, and Vanilla Ice Cream, 114
Boston Lettuce Hearts, Braised, 236
bouquet garni, 23
breakfasts
   Applesauce Cake, 76
   Cinnamon Sticky Buns, 78
   Peach Tart, Fast, 162
   Scottish Cream Scones, 77
brioche, 232
broccoli rabe, 181
Brussels sprouts, 180, 200
butter, 9, 211
Butternut Squash, Orecchiette with Lentils,
   Cream, and, 182
butternut squash risotto, 161

cabbage, 200
Caprese salad, 128–129
Caprese salad on bread, 94
caraway seeds, ideas for, 110
cardamom pods, ideas for, 110
Carrot Soufflé, 195
cauliflower, 181
Cauliflower Soup with Cumin Seeds and Parsley,
   198
Cava, 43
Champagne, 42–43
Cheese!, 38, 89, 124, 168, 219
Cheese Puffs, 210
chestnuts, 199, 201, 218
chicken, 139. *See also* meats
   Chicken, Roasted, with Watercress, 138
   Chicken Noodle Soup, 22–25
   Chicken Soup with Ginger, Barley, and
     Chestnuts, 199
   Fried Chicken, Sort of, 84
   Moroccan Pastillas, Mini, 208
Chickpeas, Spicy, 207

NOT ON LOVE ALONE

NOT ON LOVE ALONE